ADVANCE

"I warmly welcome this book on the new style of leadership, needed by organisations to survive and thrive in complex and volatile business environments. I could not agree more – it is all about people and their mindset!"

Vlatka Hlupic, author of the award-winning *The Management Shift* book

"I am a big fan of self-management for workplaces. However, as a co-founder of a self-managed company, I get very impatient with books that overhype self-management and don't spend enough time on how to get there and how to make it sustainable. Erik is a practitioner and it shows in this book. As he says, this book is not a 'codex that you must follow dogmatically'. Better than that, the book is a platform for the mindset, habits, and practices to help you create a more humane and meaningful workplace, with more engaged and happier people. Go ahead and read it."

Matt Perez, co-founder, Nearsoft Inc

"Excellent! Erik has written a book you can't put down. He takes you by the hand and leads you safely through the vast amount of academic studies and leadership literature and presents his own very attractive and consistent framework on how to shift from the Yesterday of Work to the Future of Work – as a leader, as an organization, as a human. Erik masters the art of inviting you in to the world of uncertainty and gives you a map to navigate towards the rising sun. Hint: It's all about people, curiosity and circular learning."

Jesper Rønnow Simonsen, Founder, NetworksPartners.biz, former chief executive officer in the Danish public sector

"Times are changing and the need to adapt and respond to the changes affecting our organisations is of vital importance. This book is filled with personal experiences and practical knowledge and will give you a sense of the essentials in responsive leadership from a Danish perspective."

Lene Tanggaard, Professor and Ph.D.,
Department of Communication and Psychology,
Aalborg University, Denmark

"Many leaders and organizations in this digitalized age are seeking how to lead under rapid changing circumstances. In his book, Erik gives an answer with very useful methods, tools and frameworks. If you seek to be a leader of tomorrow, let this book be one of your inspirations."

Rikke Hvilshøj, chief executive officer, Dansk IT

"Having read *The Responsive Leader* I can say that I am inspired. Erik is theoretically well founded, but many authors are that. What sets this book apart is the hands-on approach: Theories only matter if they lead to practical results. That's what this book is about. I would highly recommend it to all my colleagues doing real work with real people for real organizations."

Lars Kolind, board chairman, serial entrepreneur,
author and professor

THE
RESPONSIVE
LEADER

HOW TO BE A FANTASTIC LEADER IN
A CONSTANTLY CHANGING WORLD

**ERIK KORSVIK
ØSTERGAARD**

Published by
LID Publishing Limited
The Record Hall, Studio 204,
16-16a Baldwins Gardens,
London EC1N 7RJ, UK

524 Broadway, 11th Floor, Suite 08-120,
New York, NY 10012, US

info@lidpublishing.com
www.lidpublishing.com

A member of:

BPR
Business Publishers Roundtable

www.businesspublishersroundtable.com

© Erik Korsvik Østergaard 2018
© LID Publishing Ltd. 2018

Printed in Great Britain by TJ International
ISBN: 978-1-911498-53-7

Cover and page design: Caroline Li

THE
RESPONSIVE
LEADER

HOW TO BE A FANTASTIC LEADER IN
A CONSTANTLY CHANGING WORLD

ERIK KORSVIK
ØSTERGAARD

LONDON   MONTERREY
MADRID   SHANGHAI
MEXICO CITY BOGOTA
NEW YORK   BUENOS AIRES
BARCELONA   SAN FRANCISCO

CONTENTS

ACKNOWLEDGEMENTS

My journey into the world of new leadership paradigms was triggered and supported by a number of people, without whom I never would have gotten where I am, and this book would not exist. I owe these people my deepest respect and gratitude.

Ole Kassow at Purpose Makers, Cycling without Age, and more, for opening my eyes to a whole new understanding and approach to what organizations are and how leadership can be executed.

Jacob Bøtter and Lars Kolind, for shaping the organization WeMind, for creating the book UNBOSS, and for inspiring conversations on the modern workplace.

Alexander Kjerulf, for inspiration on happiness at work, and for pointing me towards the WorldBlu organization and community, through which I have met numerous new friends and collaborators in the world of new organization formats.

Perry Timms, for numerous conversations on Skype and Slack, and in the real world, and for pushing the agenda for an HR Transition.

Martin Ellemann Olesen at Ugilic, for great conversations and sparring over a long period on agile leadership and new paradigms for organizational teamwork.

Mikko Laukka and Jens Jakob Svanholt at Danske Bank, and the full management team and all employees in

Risk Analytics, for trusting me with the task of supporting them in the transition and further development into the world of modern and different workplaces.

Kent Højlund at Pingala, and the full Pingala team, for letting me inspire and guide them in reaching for their sky-high ambitions, and for playing along with me on the radical activities.

Max Sejbæk at ProActive, for letting me use the teams and organization as a 'lab' for some of my crazy experiments.

Peter Skjødt and Gorm Priem, also from ProActive, for being partners in exploring the mechanisms of responsive leadership in real life.

Maya Drøschler, Maiken Piil, Inge Kindberg, and Nille Skalts, for inspiration and their drive for the modern leadership agenda in Denmark.

Christian Ørsted, for strong inspiration and dialogues on leadership, and for continuous encouragement in writing this book.

Jesper Rønnow Simonsen, for a lot of mutual sparring sessions over coffee about modern leadership in the public sector.

Puk Falkenberg, for reverse-mentoring, and for a sharp eye and clear observations on change management, and on behaviour in organizations that are transforming.

All the great leaders in Novo Nordisk, NNIT, and Ørsted (prev. DONG Energy) for inspiring me on great leadership, and for entrusting me with the freedom to try new approaches.

And last but not least, Line Bloch, my business partner and wife, for support, review, comments, and endless encouragement in creating this book, and for joining forces with me to create organizations, where people want to show up for work.

FOREWORD

This book is a result of 15 years spent working in the technology and software fields, and my subsequent experiences with a range of management and leadership styles, employee profiles, and organizational structure.

I've seen rock-hard management tyrannies, and super-soft hippie-like leaders. I've experienced the dotcom bubble-burst, the financial crisis 2008-11, and the disruption movement first hand. I've been a software developer, software architect, project manager, service delivery manger, consultant, advisor, and departmental manager. I've worked in organizations with as many as 450,000 employees, and those with just two.

Most notably, I've witnessed an emerging paradigm shift in organizational leadership in the last decades of the 20th century, driven by developments in technology and society, which have changed my view on the modern workplace and the future of work.

Clearly, there is a need for a new type of leadership and organization based on relationships, purpose, value-creation, engagement, network, transparency, involvement, belonging and trust.

I absolutely approach this from a positive angle. No dooms-day here. No 'we're all losing our jobs and being replaced by robots'. There will be changes, but this book aims to help you and your organization prepare for that.

When I 'drank the Kool-Aid' in 2012 and had the epiph-any of a new leadership style, there existed only a few mod-els or tools for making the philosophy operational. I had to create new tools, codify them, test them, make mistakes, and adapt the mindset accordingly. At the time I was a departmental manager and wanted to make the everyday lives of my team fantastic.

The results couldn't be denied: Sky-high engagement. Employees with an understanding of what contribution they made, and why. Value-creation, wellbeing, and happy customers. And a more profitable business.

This book presents the learning and observations from my time as a manager of both teams and projects, and from advising and working with numerous leaders in the past decade. I'll present four key findings:

1. Five guiding principles for the future of work
2. Five areas of the future of work
3. The triple-bottom-line of responsive leadership – that is, how you measure progress and success
4. Your role and behaviour as a modern, responsive leader

To this day I'm still fascinated by technology, but I have a keener eye on the human leadership side of work now, than I had 15 years ago.

I hope you'll be inspired.

Erik Korsvik Østergaard

INTRODUCTION

i.
AN EMERGING PARADIGM SHIFT

The world is changing. The world has changed already.

The change in technology in the 20th century has driven a massive development in organizations and in society. The world has been described as volatile, uncertain, complex, and ambiguous – in short: VUCA. This demands a shift in mindset, in skillset, and in behaviour. At the same time, this is a tremendous opportunity for shaping the future.

Many organizations are trying to find their feet in the new paradigm. They need to be responsive to stay relevant to employees and to customers, and to adapt to a changing world. This so-called Fourth Industrial Revolution demands new approaches to leaders and to leadership.

However, the VUCA term is not only a negative, dystopic framing, suggesting shakiness, automation, robots, and job losses. It also offers a huge possibility for embracing work and leadership in a new way, and for addressing the development with a mindset of openness and experimentation. A positive and optimistic paradigm shift is emerging, putting engagement, relationship, inclusion, freedom, and leadership at the centre; both for employees and customers. Leaders who master this paradigm shift have to understand both methodologies, gravitate towards the new paradigm, and know how to combine and deliver – or mix and dose – them in a responsive way.

The world has changed already – but have you changed with it? Has your management group developed? Has your organization?

This book is for you, if you are a leader or wish to be one.

This book is for you, if you want to lead your organization into the 21st century.

This book is for you, if you feel bombarded with input, articles, and news about automation, the exponential growth in computer power and data, and new ways of working, but cannot grasp it and don't know where to start.

This book is for you, if you really want to make a difference in this world, and want the professional relationship between yourself and your employees to be great.

The book describes:
- A codification of the mechanisms, behaviour and mindset of the responsive leader
- A comprehensive and proven model that covers five guiding principles and the five elements of the future of work
- The characteristics of organizations in the future
- The role and behaviour of the responsive leader in the future
- How to mix the old and the new world when needed.

When you've read this book, you'll be able to:
- Understand the paradigm shift
- Understand the updated mindset
- Know where to start
- Identify and handle challenges with help from the models in the book
- Motivate your employees and peers to get started too.

ii.
THE PROCESS FOR ESTABLISHING
THE MODELS

With a background in engineering, I have a profound interest in understanding why things happen, and how events or results can be reproduced. In other words; how to codify mechanisms and understand if they are causal or correlated, and also to understand how sensitive they are to change. Does it take a small or large amount of input to make change happen? My time in university circled around mathematical modelling and simulations, and the mastered skill of pattern recognition and identifying super or sub models has been a fantastic help in doing so.

Over the five years leading up to writing this book, I've given more than 150 keynote speeches, and been engaged with more than 50 organizations and 300 leaders who wanted to transform to a modern leadership style. I've also gathered test and survey results from more than 2,500 respondents on either personal leadership style or organizational dynamics.

The work has been an ongoing cycle of a practical nature:

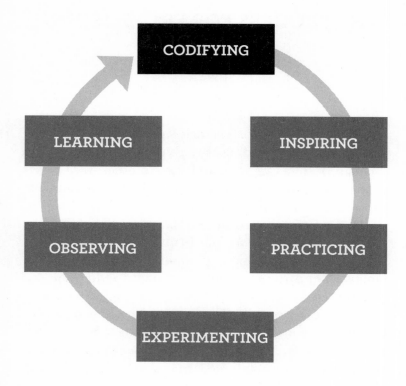

FIGURE 1

The process for establishing the models via working
with leaders, and from personal experience as a leader

- **Codifying** leadership mechanisms to describe causality or correlation, including triggers for change.
  This has typically led to a visual model or diagram,
  because it makes it easier to explain, understand,
  absorb, act and benchmark on.

- By presenting the codification and **inspiring** both leaders and employees to reflect and relate to their own situation in the light of the codification, I've gathered data on their responses (or lack of), their understanding and acknowledgement, and most of all their eagerness to act on it.
- **Practicing** the methods both myself and with my customers in my daily life as a leader. I've strived to get hands-on with the challenges, models, and approaches that we work with.
- **Experimenting** with mechanisms, tools, triggers, social balance, communication, behaviour, and, yes, even wording of sentences has been a key element in my work. This has unconsciously grown to be my *modus operandi* for practicing my trade: to not be afraid to try new things or approaches to both my own work and to the cases and customers we work with. Sometimes it leads to enormous breakthroughs. Sometimes we learn what does not work.
- **Observing** on one hand the research field, the societal development, and the simultaneous rise in comparable leadership movements across the globe; and on the other hand, the leaders and employees' reactions to the same kind of input. Not only does this provide data to reject or support a proposed codification, tool, or methodology, but it's also a constant source of inspiration and motivation
- **Learning** and humbly adjusting my beliefs and behaviour to the benefit of the purpose: to create a better understanding of the future of work and the modern workplace, and to create better codifications, that leaders and employees can and will use.
- All of which leads back to **codification**, starting the cycle once again.

Please note, that I do not claim this to be of a strict scientific nature with a peer-reviewed data foundation. It's based on numerous workshops, feedback sessions, coaching sessions, interviews, organizational transformations, and change management projects, resulting in a vast amount of operational experience and practical learning, combined with descriptive literature and studies from sources like *Harvard Business Review*, Deloitte, McKinsey, Gartner, and Centre for Futures Studies.

iii.
MY PURPOSE WITH THE BOOK

The purpose of the book is to share my experiences, learning, models, codifications, and results, so that you can be inspired to try a new leadership style and philosophy that matches the requirements of the 21st century. My intention is to light the path for you, so you can find your own way without too much fumbling.

I will not provide a finished codex that you must follow dogmatically. This is not a reference book with all the answers about leadership in the 21st century.

The focus will be on the mindset you must have as a leader, and on the behaviour and practices that can support it. The book provides a platform and several methods that will help you to understand, get started and make it happen – that is, a variant of design-thinking.

You might find yourself conflicted between your old, auto-reactions and your new, adapted behaviour. The point of this book is to shed as much light on the mindset and the paradigm shift for you to master it, to illuminate the problem, and find a solution yourself.

The book consists of three overall components:
- An in-depth description of the **MINDSET** of the future of work, the paradigm shift, and motivation for engaging in it.
- A walk-through of the **MODELS**, as applied to the domains of running an organization. You will find both comprehensive, holistic models and correlations, and analysis of the individual components.

- A description of how to dose and **MIX** the different elements, avoiding evangelism and 'going from one extreme to the other', but instead enabling you to tailor the composition based on the situation.

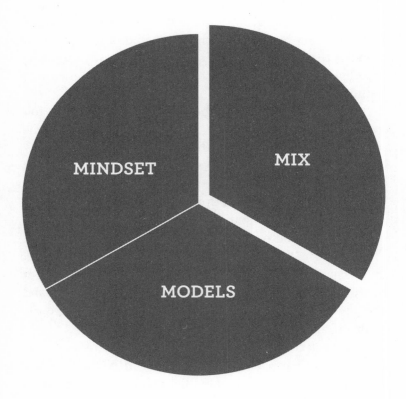

FIGURE 2

The three parts of the book: Mindset, Models, and Mix

My sincere hope is to help you understand the why, how, and what of responsive leadership. It requires that you are willing to invest the time. It requires patience. There is no quick fix. For some, a transformation can take six months before the new behaviour is well established. For others, it may take several years.

For quick reference, here is a visual summary of the four key findings in the book:

Five guiding principles

1. People first
2. Purpose, meaning, sense-making, and value-creation
3. Continuous innovation and experimentation
4. An insatiable drive for results
5. Everybody has the opportunity to take a lead

Triple-bottom-line of responsive leadership

Social Capital	Value Creation	Economic Health

FIGURE 3

An overview of the four key findings,
codifying the correlation between the models

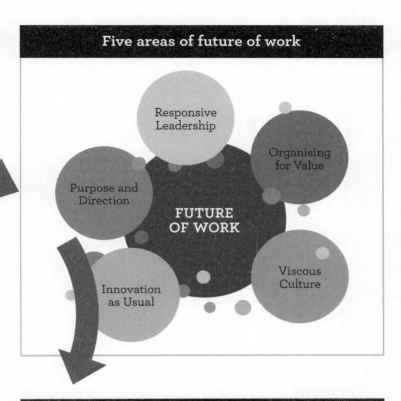

Five areas of future of work

- Responsive Leadership
- Organising for Value
- Purpose and Direction
- FUTURE OF WORK
- Innovation as Usual
- Viscous Culture

Roles and behaviour of the responsive leader

Coach and mentor	Ensures purpose	Focuses on roles and network
Entrepreneur	Challenges status quo	Measures the right things
Master of white space	Ensures delegation	Is a role model on emotional intelligence
Gardener of the ecosystem	Values collaboration	Thrives with uncertainty

PART ONE:
MINDSET

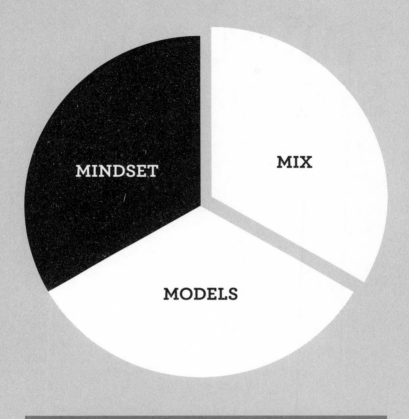

FIGURE 4

... in which we lay out the holistic mindset of the respon-sive leader, the overall approach, and the shift in gravity to achieve the approach.

1
PARADIGM SHIFT

About the emerging paradigm shift:
Why it's here, why we must take it seriously,
what effect it has, and what it means to
organizations and leaders.

We explore the shift in mindset in detail.

We look at a VUCA world, technology
trends, society shifts, and automation.
We need to be responsive in order to adapt
to a changing world and stay relevant to
employees and customers.

i.
THE WORLD HAS CHANGED

The requirements for both management and organizations have evolved continuously during the last century, correlating with advancements in psychology, the arts, music, technology, the political landscape, and society.

It's hard to put a finger on a specific time or event marking the change, but the driver and the cause of the development is often said to be technological advancement. The propagation of the internet and computers is one of the clearest vital signs of the change, since it has made global communication and access to knowledge easy.

We are always 'online'. Crowd-sourcing, artificial intelligence (AI), and automation are possible, both with robots and software. This has dramatically influenced the customer's behaviour and attitude to the market, the employee's relationship to organizations and work, and management and leaders' roles and behaviours. It has also played a role in connecting the world and enabling globalisation – supporting or even advancing societal development.

In Denmark, two major publications have come from the Centre for Futures Studies: *Anarconomy* in 2009 (Mogensen, Thomsen, et al. 2009) and *Out of Control* in 2010 (Mogensen, Møller-Elshøj, et al. 2010). They described the development that was later labelled as 'The Fourth Industrial Revolution'. Other great sources and descriptions are found in *Abundance* (Kotler and Diamandis 2012), *Exponential Organizations* (Ismail, et al. 2014), and *UNBOSS* (Kolind and Bøtter 2012), and numerous blogs and articles online by World Economic Forum (World Economic Forum 2017), SCENARIO (Center for Futures Studies 2017), and Bersin by Deloitte (Bersin 2017).

A number of megatrends are prominent:

- The search for **purpose**, meaning, and sense-making
- How we handle **relationships**, togetherness, communities, and connections, driven by online behaviour
- The presence of three or four **generations** at work simultaneously, for example Baby Boomers, Millennials, and Gen X/Y/Z/Alpha
- **Diversity** in leadership, most prominently seen as the (still too slow but yet noticeable) growth of female leaders, differences in educational and business backgrounds, in cognitive skills, and in age
- Focus on **sustainability** and the sharing economy
- Strong **urbanisation** and globalisation
- The immense advancements in science, **technology**, engineering, and mathematics (STEM), including digitalisation and automation.

In general, the speed of change in this development is constantly increasing, and is called the 'change of change'. In fact we have never seen anything like it: We are looking into a future with constant change. MORE changes, RAPID changes, and PIVOTAL changes, in technology, information, and structures (Hamel, Reinventing the Technology of Human Accomplishment 2011).

As mentioned earlier, it is said that any technological or societal change is characterised by VUCA (Wikipedia, Volatility, uncertainty, complexity and ambiguity 2017):

"VUCA is an acronym used to describe or reflect on the volatility, uncertainty, complexity and ambiguity of general conditions and situations. (...)

V = Volatility. The nature and dynamics of change, and the nature and speed of change forces and change catalysts.

U = Uncertainty. The lack of predictability, the prospects for surprise, and the sense of awareness and understanding of issues and events.

C = Complexity. The multiplex of forces, the confounding of issues, no cause-and-effect chain, and confusion that surrounds organization.

A = Ambiguity. The haziness of reality, the potential for misreads, and the mixed meanings of conditions; cause-and-effect confusion."

It is broadly accepted that VUCA behaviour has been around for thousands of years. However, as Gary Hamel and others document, the acceleration of changes is unprecedented (Hamel, Reinventing the Technology of Human Accomplishment 2011).

This means that we have a harder time justifying long, rigid plans, and there is not always one clear solution for a problem. This means that, from time to time, we must take larger risks and experiment more. This means that life as a leader or employee might be filled with constant doubt and worry if we don't handle this properly.

BUT, this also means that we can change our approach to work and leadership in a new, positive, optimistic way. The VUCA framing is a possibility for a paradigm shift, making way for new approaches to distributed leadership and handling uncertainty via a conscious approach. This is absolutely an optimistic, positive approach.

Please note, that I write 'harder', 'not always', 'from time to time', and 'can be'. We have to be careful with dogmatic claims, which is exactly one of the premises for the world we're describing. Instead we must understand and describe the leadership and organizations that can embrace and exploit this, while at the same time care for each other.

All these changes provide both challenges and possibilities.

People who see challenges alone, fail.
People who see possibilities alone, fail.
People who see challenges AND
possibilities, win.

Paraphrased from Costa Markides
(Markides 2015)

We must fundamentally shift our mindset and behaviour. THIS is the paradigm shift, and it's a positive one.

Kenneth Mikkelsen and Richard Martin describe the approach in their book *The Neo-Generalist* (Mikkelsen and Martin 2016): we must create a shift in mind, skills, behaviour and systems; leading to a shift in culture.

From working with leaders in the past decade, I'm convinced it must happen in that order. First, and most important, is the mindset, mentality and philosophy, which is also the main focus in the book. If you change, develop, and align your mindset in the organization, and together create an evolvement in new skills (both organizational and personal skills), then the change in behaviour will be a natural consequence of the mindset.

It would be a mistake if I created a list of 'do this and act like that' for you, for several reasons. First, that would be contradictory to the fundamental premise of an ever-changing world. Such a list might quickly become outdated. Second, any such list requires a context to live in; a context that you and your team will be the only ones to know and understand. Finally, if you comply with such a list without understanding the mindset, you will not have the possibility to freestyle and handle conflicts. This is the most important factor of all: you must be able to ping-pong with the mindset and derive the best possible behaviour based on the situation at hand.

It starts and ends with the mindset.

ii.
WHY WORRY? WHY CARE?

Let's look at some facts about organizations, leadership and employees in the modern workplace and in the future of work, in order to understand the importance of and the need for a paradigm shift.

One vital sign is low employee engagement. It has been thoroughly investigated and documented, for example by Gallup (Gallup, Employee Engagement in U.S. Stagnant in 2015 2016), that 50-70% of the workforce is disengaged. This is an enormous number of employees and managers. Almost unanimously, the studies have found that work, to a certain degree, is meaningless, not fun, and without freedom. Some even report a fear at work, both due to the manager's way of instilling anxiety and a culture of zero tolerance towards failure, and due to the fear of losing their job to a robot or a piece of software.

McKinsey reported (McKinsey 2017) that 40% of our working hours are in scope for being automated or phased out over a 20-year period, with technology that already exists. In 2013, the University of Oxford made a list of 702 jobs and their probability for being 'computerizable' (Frey and Osborne 2013): more than 300 of these had more than 80% probability for being automated.

In 2016, Bloch&Østergaard and DARE2 (Østergaard and Østergaard 2016) conducted a study with 900 respondents in Denmark, the UK, and the US, which documented that only 18% of Danes believe it's likely that their current job will be replaced by new technology (e.g. computers, robots, software). In the US, it was 30%. In the UK, 31%. So there is a significant cultural variation in the understanding, severity and focus of the issue.

It is also said that many of the jobs our children will have in the future are not invented yet (Aakerberg 2016). And that, "Half a century ago, the life expectancy of a firm in the Fortune 500 was around 75 years. Now it's less than 15 years and declining even further." (Denning 2011)

The World Economic Forum has predicted the top 10 skills to master in 2020 (A. Gray 2016), which proposes a heavy blend of creative and innovative thinking, entrepreneurial problem solving, and emotional intelligence (EQ).

We're facing some radical changes, but it is not all doom and gloom.

Despite the seemingly dystopic predictions of AI, automation and loss of jobs, these changes bring some exciting possibilities for replacing the existing management and organizational structures with something more modern and future-oriented. The development and progress makes this the right time to stop and rethink our approach to work. This is an optimistic possibility.

This is where the paradigm shift enters the picture.

iii.
WHAT DOES IT TAKE?

We need a completely new approach to work. We need to be able to respond to the many rapid changes. We need new skills, new behaviours, and new systems. Most of all we need a new holistic mindset for handling a new type of workplace. Overall, we can see this shift as a focus from **doing** stuff to **being** someone.

A central element is the focus on creating value versus creating money. The more we look in the direction of abundance of products and results, the less interesting it is to focus on money as the goal. Money is a result, not a reason to exist (Sinek, Start With Why 2009). Instead we seek to create value for our employees, our customers, our community, and our society. This 'value-creation' is the new currency.

The design of our workplace, and our understanding of what constitutes 'work' must change too:

More	Less
People and culture	People are resources
Delegation and mandate	Top-down-control
Extreme transparency	Keeping things private
Experiments	Planning
Complex thinking	Simple solutions
Exception-based work	Job-and-task orientation
I belong here	I work here

We will see a transformation in HR: in attitude, philosophy, structure, service offerings, and skillset. This will be the result of three things:

1. We stop looking at humans as resources, but instead look at people and culture as a core of our approach to each other. Our employees are not production resources; they are human beings with personal lives, experiences, histories, and attitudes. They shape our culture, and thus who we are and how we do things.

2. The line of business has for a long time looked outside the organization for support on strategic leadership and organizational development (OD). This is going to change. HR – or should we say People and Culture – will regain the position as vendors of leadership and OD.

3. The automation shift makes it easier to outsource the more functional tasks in HR like candidate screening, profiling, legal support etc.

We will see a transformation in the amount of freedom in organizations, removing hierarchies and control, replacing it with networks, gig workers, trust, and freedom.

We will see a transformation in the work-job-task mix, with the entry of automation and software robots which can handle routine tasks and processes, enabling us to handle all the things that are exceptions to the rules.

Finally, **we'll see emerging organizations that are extremely visionary and ambitious**, rooted in strong human values and focused on creating value for customers and society, while at the same time being very profitable. These organizations will not necessarily be large companies, since size and impact are not causal to each other.

Several organizations and movements have described frameworks for this already, which have been applied with varying success and output. See for example, B Corp, Conscious Capitalism, Holacracy, Responsive Org., Teal, and WorldBlu Freedom At Work.

All science and study on organizational change management shows that the engagement and participation of top management is crucial for the success of the transformation. That's why you, and your role as manager and leader, are the most important element in this paradigm shift. You are the one who points the organization and your employees in the right direction and towards the right mindset. And it's you who needs to take the first step. And the next, and the next, and to ensure that you do it together and that no one is left behind.

Yes, technology is the premise and the driver, but the future is all about relationships, network, value-creation, adaptability, and responsiveness. People first. The great part is that it creates engagement and joy at work, while productivity is kept high. (See for example (Sheridan 2013), (Kjerulf 2014), and (Stewart 2012).)

Organizations must establish a framework for constant adaptation and agility, nurturing and exploiting responsiveness.

2

THE FIVE GUIDING PRINCIPLES FOR THE FUTURE OF WORK

The guiding principles behind the future of work are the foundation for everything, and what you base the mindset and all subsequent skills, behaviour, elements, tools, and actions on.

Here we look at the **first key finding**, namely the **five guiding principles**, one by one.

The modern and responsive leaders I have worked with and observed all have a handful of behaviours in common. Correlating this with the dominant leadership literature from the past decade, and with emerging leadership frameworks, a pattern emerges for the mindset and the future of work.

As I explained earlier, we are living in a world with both challenges and huge possibilities. You will be less successful if you remain doing what you are used to doing, and if you plan the future thoroughly and in detail without adapting frequently.

The guiding principles of the future of work and responsive leadership embrace this ever-changing world, and provide safety for the organization and its employees. This is done by focusing on distributed leadership and exploiting the huge opportunities of uncertainty in an optimistic, experimental way:

The five guiding principles for the future of work

1. People first
2. Purpose, meaning, sense-making, and value-creation
3. Continuous innovation and experimentation
4. An insatiable drive for results
5. Everybody has the opportunity to take a lead

This chapter describes the principles as they are introduced and executed by the leaders I've observed. During the rest of the book, we'll apply the principles to the five areas of the modern workplace and go into more detail.

Also see the case studies in this book from Danske Bank, Pingala, and ProActive, illustrating how the leaders and organizations embrace and live by the guiding principles.

i.
PEOPLE FIRST

Technology is a driver for development, efficiency and creativity, when it comes to providing ever better solutions and products. Still, the interactions, decisions, and business transactions hinge around **people** and the relationships between people. You are not a B2B or a B2C company, you are H2H – human to human.

People first is a principle that applies in many aspects:
- Towards yourself
- Towards employees
- Towards customers
- Towards community
- Towards society.

Note, it is not 'customers first' or 'employees first'. It is people. You should care about the people you are engaging with, working with, helping, providing services to, and doing business with.

To put it clearly, relationships beat skills. The Massachusetts Institute of Technology (MIT) and the Technical University of Denmark (DTU) have both documented this (de Montjoye, et al. 2014): teams that are created based on relationships outperform teams that are created based on skills. In the old days, you competed on skills and price alone. Now, relationships give you the competitive edge, in addition to being skilful and mastering your trade.

ii.
PURPOSE, MEANING, SENSE-MAKING, AND VALUE-CREATION

In a quickly changing and evolving world, we also naturally grasp for what does *not* change, namely our deeply rooted need for things to make sense. This unfolds in two dimensions, firstly for the company, and secondly on a personal level.

For the company – and hence for the organization and the customers – the purpose is the gravity point that enables us to focus our engagement and understand our identity. This is even more important in a world that constantly evolves. We need to have our core mission statement and purpose behind every action and as a defining identity for the organization. What we are, what value we create, and what problems we solve are the non-changing gravity point for our organization.

As Deloitte says (Deloitte, 2017 Deloitte Global Human Capital Trends 2017), we need to address and embrace new technology and skills every four to five years. Constant shifts and shakes in the market landscape occur, both from the volatile economic market and the customer's innovative competition. Our identity and 'this is why we exist as a company' is the bedrock for our activities. This comes from purpose and meaningfulness together.

On the employee level, the everyday connection to the purpose can be difficult and short-lived. It can be hard, even impossible at times, to see how everyday mundane tasks help the company to achieve the purpose. This is where meaningfulness and sense-making plays a vital role: From the employee level, sense-making and meaningfulness in tasks and interactions are motivators for engagement and for understanding that they provide value and contribute to the context they are in.

As such, it is the leaders' responsibility to close the disconnect between the purpose and the employees. This is done through a focus on value-creation for each person and task. As one C-level executive phrases it: work must make sense. It must be meaningful. We must create value, not just money.

The responsive leader ensures purpose and meaningfulness in all actions, and for everything.

iii.
CONTINUOUS INNOVATION
AND EXPERIMENTATION

"Whoever tries the most stuff, wins," as Tom Peters wrote in his book *Excellence Now: Action* (Peters 2015).

A guiding principle for work in the future is that you need to experiment much more than you used to. In a world that changes rapidly, and where there are several 'right' answers to a question, you must experiment, test, and investigate deliberately. Inspect and adapt.

Naturally, the responsive leader needs to be innovative with products and processes; both key processes and support processes. However, you also need to be innovative and drive experimentation with your leadership, your mechanisms for engaging with others, and your organizational dynamics. You need to be innovative with your innovation.

You need to move your comfort zone from maintenance mode to one of balanced risk-taking, using both everyday increments and iterations, and strategic initiatives. This requires curiosity, a drive for creation, and acceptance of mistakes.

The responsive leader is innovative, and is experimental in their approach to themselves, to their employees, to their organization, to business, and to their customers.

iv.
AN INSATIABLE DRIVE
FOR RESULTS

Some think, incorrectly, that a people-and-purpose ori-ented leadership paradigm will not lead to results, or will have a laissez-faire approach to making money. These assumptions are wrong. The responsive leader balances the financial-, production-, and people-oriented results, like the social capital and the value you create. Production results must not be reached at the cost of wellbeing for themselves, their employees, peer leaders, or customers.

On top of the focus on interpersonal activities, the leaders of the future have a resilient drive for results, which propa-gates and spreads to employees, colleagues, and peer leaders.

Results in this context unfold in several aspects, reflected mostly by the individual leader's personal profile, and the role they take as either a professional or social lead.

Some results are tangible, related to the three Ps of pro-duction: products, processes, and projects. These are meas-ured via productivity, efficiency, deadlines, quality, cost, and revenue.

Some are intangible, related to relationships, people, and teams. These results are harder to measure as they are personal, subjective, and highly biased by interpretation. Results and value-creation in this area comes in the form of trust, engagement, personal development, courage, col-laboration, flexibility, wellbeing, and joy.

Common to these areas is the insatiable drive for results; for engaging in actions that have measurable and validated learning, milestones, quantities, or qualities.

V.
EVERYBODY HAS THE OPPORTUNITY TO TAKE A LEAD

The final guiding principle in the future of work is that everybody has the opportunity to take a lead.

You cannot rely on yourself to be the sole source of ideas, plans, decisions, and communication. In the future, it is even more evident than before that the hierarchy and the silos must be augmented with networked teams, and that engagement force and decision power must be distributed.

Previously, an organization was designed for functional optimisation, with leaders being specialists in their functional areas. Now, there is no reason to assume that you as the leader are the smartest, the wisest, the one with the most relevant experience or the most influencer power.

Each of these capabilities might reside in employees all across the organization. To stay relevant to both employees and customers, we need to engage those people who have the will, skill, ability, and drive to run with an idea and make it happen. The responsive leader enables everybody to take the lead, and ensures at the same time that proper support, motivation, and instruction are in place to help an employee who might be new or not fully schooled in the area. This was first described in 1969 as Situational Leadership (Hersey and Blanchard 1969).

Additionally, you have an obligation to enable people to grow. The future of work is a world of possibilities that requires you to be curious and to be a creator. This will not happen if you do not get the best out of people, and enable them to take a chance, commit to a task, receive feedback, and be proud of the results they achieve; either intrapersonal achievements, like self-worth and self-esteem; interpersonal achievements, like relationship and trust; or mastery of skills and processes.

The responsive leader takes it upon themselves to enable others to lead; to come up with ideas, make decisions, and drive the organization forward. Employees in the future want to lead, and want to lead now (paraphrased from Ali Hall's talk at Presidents' Summit, (Hall 2016)).

vi.
SUMMARY

The transformative leaders I've worked with in the past decade have all had similar approaches to leadership.

I observed that their personal development and growth into being responsive leaders had the same characteristics, which are explained in detail in chapter 9iv:

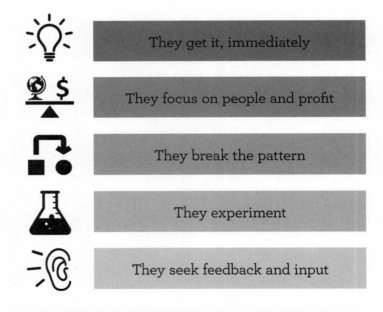

They get it, immediately

They focus on people and profit

They break the pattern

They experiment

They seek feedback and input

FIGURE 5

The traits of leaders that transform: How they think and act

It also became clear, by codifying their behaviour, that they discovered or applied **the five guiding principles** to their work:

1. People first
2. Purpose, meaning, sense-making, and value-creation
3. Continuous innovation and experimentation
4. An insatiable drive for results
5. Everybody has the opportunity to take a lead.

In the next part of the book we apply the guiding principles to the five areas of work, to describe the future of strategy, innovation, culture, organizing, and leadership.

3

THE WORLD OF NEW LEADERSHIP PARADIGMS

We take a look at why managers are reluctant or hesitant to get started – and what we can do to light up the path they need to follow.

We also take a short look at some of the new leadership frameworks that you can use for inspiration.

i.
WHERE SHOULD YOU
START THE JOURNEY?

Over the past few years I have not met a single manager who did *not* know that the role of the leader and the definition of the modern workplace is changing, and that something new is needed. Managers are being confronted by it in the newspapers, online, at conferences, from their own managers, the board of directors, the shareholders, their employees, their customers, and their competitors ... but some of them have a difficult time getting started.

Despite the bombardment of input, many managers still have their focus on existing goals, their well-known habits and style of working, and the direction they have already made. They are skilled in fine-tuning their machines and business units, creating a more and more efficient and effective production apparatus, brilliantly designed for creating what they also created yesterday. The challenge is that yesterday's products and processes might not be suitable or in demand tomorrow. Changing habits, leadership style and structures requires resources, time, and effort.

When you address this issue in front of managers, they reply that they are fully aware of the dilemma, but that they'll get to it "when our project is done" or "after the annual fiscal closure" ... which is then hijacked by the next year's strategy seminar and planning.

The explanation – or excuse, if you like – is time constraints; either bad timing or lack of time. It never seems to be a lack of will, skill, ability, or interest. However, once we dig a little and get to speak to them one-on-one, the anxiety of not knowing what to do, or where to start, becomes painfully clear. They are often also afraid of the imposter syndrome, of not having the skills or the courage, and being incapable of handling the future and having a role in it.

One observation from my work with leaders is that the first step is to 'lighten the path' for them. Show the new paradigm, the reason for engaging in it, share examples and case studies, show the methods, and talk about the challenge of the 'leap of faith'.

The leaders who transform first – and pull the rest with them – already have it in them. What is needed are some guiding principles, tons of inspiration, and frequent encouragement.

You can make a huge difference by taking the first step. Seek out case studies and inspiration for yourself, your employees and your management peers, and take the leap. It's all about looking in a new direction, and being willing to take it.

What matters is that you stop, reflect, change direction, and invest time. It only happens if you do something different today than you did yesterday.

ii.
NAVIGATING THE WORLD OF NEW LEADERSHIP FRAMEWORKS

Several new leadership styles and organizational designs have emerged as a result of the paradigm shift and the global megatrends. Here are a few:

Responsive Org. (Responsive.Org 2017) describes different characteristics of organizations with five sliders, each spanning a spectrum of opposite characteristics, e.g. profit vs. purpose, hierarchies vs. networks, controlling vs. empowering, planning vs. experimentation, and privacy vs. transparency.

Holacracy (Holacracy 2017) is organization form without hierarchy, but is instead based on a self-organized and self-managed network, and mechanisms for solving problems.

Conscious Capitalism (Conscious Capitalism 2017) and **B Corp** (Bcorporation.net 2017) are organization styles focusing on balancing purpose and profit, to the benefit of employees, stakeholders, and society.

WorldBlu and their "Freedom at Work" describes a philosophy for democratic organizations based on ten principles (WorldBlu, WorldBlu 2017), leading to freedom, engagement, safety, and trust in the workplace:

1. Purpose + Vision
2. Transparency
3. Dialogue + Listening
4. Fairness + Dignity
5. Accountability
6. Individual + Collective

7. Choice
8. Integrity
9. Decentralisation
10. Reflection + Evaluation.

This book describes the kind of leader that knows when to combine and incorporate these new leadership frameworks with the existing, old school style with deliberate care, to the benefit of customers, employees, and society: The Responsive Leader.

PART TWO:
MODELS

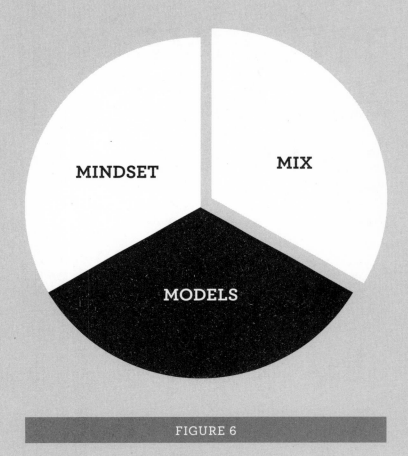

FIGURE 6

... in which we study all elements in the future of work via codification of experiences, models, tools, processes, and case studies.

4
THE FIVE AREAS OF FUTURE OF WORK

Introducing the **second key finding**, namely a model for engaging in the transformation, covering **five areas of future of work**:

Purpose and direction, innovation, culture, organizing, and leadership.

The future of work is characterised simultaneously by an adjusted and holistic approach. This is the second key finding in the book, which we'll unfold in the next chapters too.

An adjusted approach, because the paradigm shift is a fundamental change to how we think and act in the workplace.

There is a drive to take a stand against the existing methodology and instead embrace the new world. Additionally, there is a clear business need to redesign and rethink work to stay relevant to customers as well as to employees. Customers seek convenience and relevancy. Employees seek immediate empowerment and development. This is even stronger with Millennials and the Gen X/Y/Z in organizations (see for example Søren Schultz Hansen (Hansen 2015) and YoungConsult (YoungConsult 2017)).

A holistic approach, because the elements of the modern workplace interlock and affect each other.

First: You cannot assume causality, but you must see the two approaches as correlated. A small change to any of the elements will affect or cause changes to one or more of the others.

Secondly: The holistic approach applies to your mindset too, and to the way you approach your personal development. You cannot start with one element or one area. You must work with all five at the same time.

By applying the five guiding principles (see Chapter 2) of the future in the modern workplace, we specifically get the **five areas of future of work**, which we'll dive into in the next chapters:

- Purpose and direction
- Innovation as usual
- Viscous culture
- Organizing for value
- Responsive Leadership.

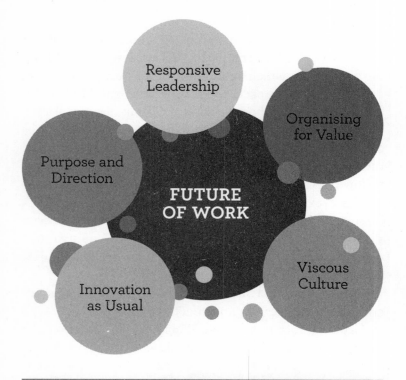

FIGURE 7

The five areas of Future of Work

These characteristics are codifications of the approach and behaviour seen in the organizations I've worked with and studied. These leaders have applied new thinking and mechanisms to the traditional areas of running and developing a business, and have managed to evolve both themselves and their organizations to be responsive to change.

Let's look at the areas, one by one.

5
PURPOSE AND DIRECTION

Say goodbye to the classic three-year, detail-oriented strategy. Say hello to purpose and direction as a supplement, or even a replacement at times.

This chapter covers purpose, meaningfulness, value-creation (functional, emotional, and societal), the role in motivation, and a balanced view on updating and adjusting the actions weekly, monthly, and yearly.

We look at the **third key finding**, namely the **triple-bottom-line of responsive leadership**.

We introduce an alternative strategic model, as a supplement or replacement for the strategy paper, balanced score-cards, and waterfall project plans.

i.
PURPOSE AND DIRECTION

In a constantly fast-changing world you cannot make thorough plans for the future of your organization by merely analysing, thinking, and planning; as if your assumptions are correct and non-changing.

Forget the classic three-year strategy documents and processes. Get rid of the urge to carry on as usual (which is: gather a strategy team, relocate to an offsite location for three days, lay detailed plans for the following years based on assumptions, go into thinking mode for two weeks afterwards, seeking opinions from the usual organizational experts, and then shift into execution mode with close monitoring, business reviews, and action plans if things don't go as forecasted).

Instead, you must focus on your purpose, your cause and belief, and your reason to exist as an organization. Understand what problems you are solving and for whom, and what value you are creating for the customers. The purpose should be the grounding for the strategy, and is an immensely strong supplement for the strategic and tactical planning.

There are three reasons for that.

One: Focusing on purpose enables you, the organization, and every employee, to focus on WHY you do what you do, instead of WHAT you do. This creates a deeper understanding and engagement, and is a perfect framework for empowerment, delegation, and commitment. If everybody understands why you do what you do, you have a foundation for challenging the status quo, for holistic thinking, and for taking initiative in a decentralised way.

Two: Focusing on purpose enables you to set the direction properly. To replace and substitute operational or tactical elements in your organization as you go along, keeping the long-term goal at the forefront. You must rethink the strategy and make it agile and circular – or spiralling – instead.

Three: Focusing on purpose is a tremendous motivation, and a filtering factor for more and more people when they choose which company to work for. This is even more evident when working with Millennials (Gallup (Gallup, How Millennials Want to Work and Live 2016) and Young-Consult (YoungConsult 2017)). With a purpose to support one or more of the 17 UN Sustainable Goals (UN 2017), it is even easier to understand and document what value you are creating and for whom, perhaps even in the daily mundane tasks, far from C-level or the customers.

The execution of the activities to support the purpose should focus on problem solving and happen in sprints with continuous adjustment of approach, technology, and speed.

ii.
THE TRIPLE-BOTTOM-LINE
OF RESPONSIVE LEADERSHIP

A key observation is that this leads to the emergence of a triple-bottom-line in the new organizations, strongly promoted by having a purpose:

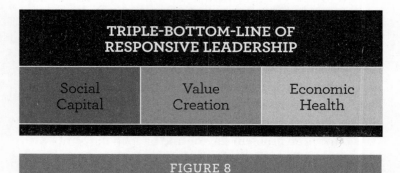

TRIPLE-BOTTOM-LINE OF RESPONSIVE LEADERSHIP

Social Capital	Value Creation	Economic Health

FIGURE 8

The Triple-bottom-line of responsive leadership

Responsive leaders and modern workplaces start focusing on these three things equally, but address them in order, mentioning economic ambitions and results last. This has been the case in Danske Bank, in Pingala, and in ProActive. Here, the leaders routinely measure and nurture the social capital via network analysis and relationship focus, and articulate a strong desire for value-creation and meaningfulness in all activities, both internally and externally. Value-creation is a KPI for a growing number of organizations.

For some employees, it's hard to understand the effect their work has on economic results, as the actual money transactions happen somewhere else in the organization, and the transparency and direct relation to their work can be extremely hard to establish. Instead, more employees, project managers, and department leads are turning to social capital and value-creation for a means of understanding the cause and effect of activities.

- **Social capital**: how strong our relationships and networks are, and what are they based on
- **Value-creation**: monitoring what kind of value the organization creates, for whom, and how much
- **Economic health**: turnover, revenue, billability etc.

"Social Capital is a form of economic and cultural capital in which
- *social networks are central,*
- *transactions are marked by reciprocity, trust, and cooperation,*
- *and market agents produce goods and services not mainly for themselves, but for a common good."*

Wikipedia (Wikipedia, Social capital 2017).

Robert Putnam defines social capital as "connections among individuals – social networks and the norms of reciprocity and trustworthiness that arise from them." (Putnam 2000).

A purpose narrative establishes correlation between the elements in the triple-bottom-line once the connection is created:

- The purpose ties you together, strengthening your relationships and social capital
- The purpose describes the value you create
- The purpose supports you in reaching your financial goals by focusing and prioritising your resources and investments.

The triple-bottom-line also embraces the elements that are documented to create happiness at work, namely relationships and meaningful results (Kjerulf 2014).

iii.
THE GREAT DISCONNECT FROM THE COMPANY STRATEGY

Why do you go to work? What drives you? And why should anybody care about your organization and your products?

Over the past ten years I've heard numerous employees – people on the frontline, highly trained specialists, and executives – say that they really don't understand their company's strategy and why they do what they do.

I started gathering data on the reasoning for this disconnect, and here are the most frequently mentioned thoughts:

Lack of clear direction: "I don't understand the direction and the reasoning for it. It does not make sense to me."

Lack of involvement: "Management does not listen to our experience, nor to our input. We have good learnings from new tools, technological solutions, and applications that we should be able to apply, but the decisions have been made already."

Lack of meaningful goals: "I don't understand why we fight for that kind of revenue, narrow-mindedly. I don't want to go to work and make money, just so that my managers can get a bigger car."

Lack of feedback loops: "Management does not see what I see. I have the daily contact with the customers, and the managers simply don't understand the situations and the challenges that we're dealing with. And they do not know how we're doing when it comes to wellbeing."

Lack of responsiveness: "I can see many possibilities for new services that would help our customers, including new technology. But the strategy is already carved in stone, so changing it is not possible."

Several issues are at play here, all of which must be addressed and seen in a new light by shifting your approach to strategy. This applies when it comes to establishing it, involving people in it, communicating it, executing it, and handling feedback and changes to it.

Some would argue that it's just a matter of strengthening the current strategy communication process. I'd argue that it would be treating symptoms only and not dealing with the root-cause, namely the **disconnect** between the employees and the organization's core, the identity, and the reason to exist. It will not solve the fundamental challenge of engagement and commitment.

If you focus on your purpose, your cause and belief (as Simon Sinek phrases it (Sinek, Start With Why 2009)), and your reason to exist as an organization; if you understand what problem you are solving, and for whom, and what value you are creating for the customers; if you communicate that narrative to everyone and invite everyone to participate in moulding and forming it; if you make sure that you fight for more than just revenue and market share, but also fight for value-creating for your customers and for society – then the disconnect will close, and the engagement will rise.

There are three reasons for engaging in an inspiring and value-creating purpose:

1. Your organization's purpose is your foundation for existence, and shifts your focus from WHAT to WHY. This creates a framework for holistic understanding everywhere in the organization, and for your community, society, and customers.

2. Maintaining this focus on purpose enables – and forces – you to adjust, stop, and agilely redesign your activities, so that you always engage in the best possible tasks and projects, with suitable technologies and methods.

3. The purpose and the unstoppable inertia for meaningfulness and value-creation is a tremendous motivation for employees, and for the business partners you surround yourself with.

There is, from time to time, a semantic and somewhat energy-wasting debate around the difference between a purpose and a mission/vision statement. These two can be used interchangeably only if the phrase or term or descriptor is (a) focused on value-creation, not skills or size or similar, (b) oriented towards what you do for others, like solving problems or enabling possibilities, (c) clearly describing who it is for, and (d) something you can turn into a touching, meaningful, and relevant narrative, for employees, customers, and community.

A purpose describes what the organization is and fights for, and for whom. It describes the problems you are solving and the value you create, not the products you make.

iv.
FACTS ABOUT PURPOSE
AND MEANINGFULNESS

Let's look at a couple of documented studies on the cause and effect of purpose and meaningful work.

Simon Sinek published *Start with Why* (Sinek, Start With Why 2009) in 2009 and created with that a strong movement of **purpose**-driven leadership. He is one of the main influencers of a structured approach, and supports this codification with numerous case studies and with a neuro-scientific description of how the brain works. He followed the success with *Leaders eat Last* (Sinek, Leaders Eat Last: Why Some Teams Pull Together and Others Don't 2014), and went even deeper into the neuro-science aspect. These two books are strongly recommended reads.

Sinek suggests that starting with your core **purpose** – the WHY – is a main factor for motivation, engagement, and successful communication.

In 2015 and 2016, The Danish labour union Krifa, together with the Happiness Research Institute and TNS Gallup, published a research paper, *God Arbejdslyst*, on motivation and what makes a good workplace. In it, they documented (Krifa 2016) that **meaningfulness** at work was, for the second year in a row, the factor that had the largest effect on the Danes' happiness at work: *"The perception of meaningfulness is so important, that it affects our perception of happiness at work more than salary, results, and colleagues put together. Or 6.5 times more than salary alone."* We explore the connection between purpose and meaningfulness in section vi.

Daniel Pink showed and documented in *Drive: The surprising truth about what motivates us* (Pink 2009) how intrinsic motivation based on autonomy, mastery, and **purpose** is far stronger, deeper, and longer lasting than extrinsic motivation from titles, rewards, and compensation.

Catherine Bailey and Adrian Madden published in *MIT Sloan Management Review* the results of a study, indicating that **meaningful work** is a self-transcendent, poignant, episodic, reflective, and personal experience (Bailey and Madden 2016).

Gallup documented in 2016 (Gallup, How Millennials Want to Work and Live 2016), that Millennials want to work for companies that fight for something more than just revenue; they want purpose in their work. YoungConsult confirmed this in a study in 2017 (YoungConsult 2017).

And, according to a study by Paul J. Sak et al., "Experiments show that having a sense of higher purpose stimulates oxytocin production, as does trust. Trust and purpose then mutually reinforce each other, providing a mechanism for extended oxytocin release, which produces happiness" (Sak 2017).

A purpose-driven organization also creates more money. Simon Caulkin published an article in the *Financial Times*, documenting that *"Companies with a purpose beyond profit tend to make more money"* (Caulkin 2016). This has also been documented by WorldBlu in their report from 2015 (WorldBlu, Freedom At Work: Growth And Resilience 2015), showing that being purpose-driven can result in up to seven times higher revenue growth compared to companies on the S&P 500 Index.

Purpose and meaningfulness are tied closely together, and as a unit they are a crucial part of the shared and co-created identity of a company. It's the purpose that draws you closer and facilitates your narrative, and with that in mind you can create meaningful work and actions.

v.
DISCOVERING AND DESCRIBING YOUR PURPOSE

Describing your purpose statement is a process that can be cumbersome, long-lasting, and filled with impediments. It unfolds in four phases:
1. Shift the mindset
2. Investigate and interview
3. Phrase it
4. Live it.

Shift the mindset to one of awareness, which promotes a desire for having an ambitious and bold purpose, instead of the classic strategy-phrases.

Seek out inspiration from the sources and studies who fact-check and document the psychology and business reasoning for having a purpose. See, for example, the sources in section iv.

It's important to get the top management and key influencers that are part of the process on board with this. Be curious about the new input, and be willing to experiment with a new approach in setting direction, ambition, and speed.

Investigate and interview key stakeholders within and outside of the company to gather input, and collaborate on finding and describing actions that support the purpose and describe the identity of the company and culture. Look for examples and case studies where the organization/company has provided non-monetary value, created possibilities, or solved problems for its customers.

Answer these questions, both as seen from inside your organization, and from the outside:
- What problem are you solving?
- For whom?
- What value are you creating?
- Why do you go to work?
- What do you believe?
- You believe the world needs ... what?
- Your purpose is ... what?

The cumbersome task of wording and phrasing the purpose means you can end up in endless discussions about a plural, or the subtle difference between 'enabling' and 'empowering'.

One way of phrasing it and getting the discussion going, is to try to build a sentence like this:

We [insert a verb, or a phrase with a verb],
so that [insert a role]
can [insert a goal or ability].

One might recognise that the structure of the sentence is inspired by User Stories and the Scrum methodology (Sutherland 2014).

A good purpose statement frames everything you do, makes sense to your customers, is unselfish, and helps you succeed. Let it sink in. Get feedback from your employees, your colleagues, your peer leaders. Get feedback from your customers and community. Does it make sense to them? Is it meaningful?

Remember that a purpose statement underlines what you do, which is to the benefit of somebody else.

Bring the purpose to life by actively using it for prioritising, motivation, setting direction, measuring progress, celebrations, and acknowledgements.

- Use it in presentations
- For motivation
- For prioritisation
- To say yes and no to projects and tasks
- To measure progress
- For evaluation and feedback
- To create identity and understanding.

I've worked with companies that have spent months aligning opinions, attitudes, and approaches to the question: what are we, and what do we fight for?

Some companies dig deep down to the roots and heritage of the founders and the initial motive for starting the company. Others grasp the opportunity to re-evaluate the reason for existing in the light of the current and future market place and demands, despite a maybe 15- or 50-year history with products and customers. Others again (and these are normally the most progressive and open-minded companies), turn to their customers and community to ask what the company does for them, thus discovering what kind of company they are perceived to be by their customers.

A good purpose statement immediately answers these questions:

Why does this organization exist?
Why should anyone care?
Why do you go to work?

Just like a mission/vision-statement, a purpose statement is concerned with what you fight for. A purpose statement describes what you will, do, and are. It does not care about what you can.

Thank you to Allan Ebdrup (Ebdrup 2017) at Debitoor for strong inspiration on this approach.

FIGURE 9

A purpose statement is concerned with what you fight for.
A purpose statement describes what you will, do, and are

vi.
THE DIFFERENCE BETWEEN PURPOSE AND MEANINGFULNESS

One of the most criticised elements of purpose-driven organizations and leadership is that it can be very hard for employees to see how their individual actions and daily work ties in to the overall purpose or mission/vison of the company.

This is where the term meaningfulness comes into play. By connecting it with the focus on value-creation we can make the ends meet, ensuring engagement, motivation, and an understanding of connectedness to the company.

Referring to a study by LRN (Forbes 2017), PWC found (PWC 2016) that "only 29% of employees in large organizations described their leadership as exhibiting an ability to 'enlist all employees in a commitment to a shared purpose,' compared with 38% of employees in medium-sized organizations and 42% of employees in smaller ones."

In other words, **it's tough to scale purpose**. This is exactly why meaningfulness and sense-making is complementary to purpose, and allows the employees to connect with their daily work and with the organization.

According to the previously mentioned study by Catherine Bailey and Adrian Madden, (Bailey and Madden 2016) **meaningful work** is a self-transcendent, poignant, episodic, reflective, and personal experience. These elements of meaningful work are to be found in the organization, the job, the task, and through interactions with others.

Based on our work with companies and organizations over the past decade, meaningfulness and sense-making come in two flavours – rational meaning and emotional meaning – and on several levels. Does this make sense to me? Is the task meaningful? Does it make sense in the team, for the company, for the customer, and for society?

It is much easier to debate meaningfulness than purpose, and the exercise is even more fruitful when you tie it into a discussion of value-creation.

Purpose is a top-down invitation, value-creation is a bottom-up experience, and meaningfulness is the glue between the two.

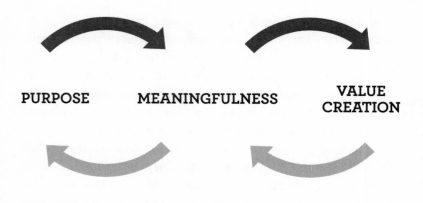

PURPOSE   **MEANINGFULNESS**   **VALUE CREATION**

FIGURE 10

The relationship between purpose, meaningfulness, and value-creation

vii.
MEASURING YOUR VALUE-CREATION

The responsive leader – and organizations that live by the philosophies of the modern workplace – places purpose on the same level as profit. They go to work to solve problems and create value for their relationships, and thus create profit and results. B Corp and Conscious Capitalism are two such approaches and philosophies that believe in doing well by doing good.

The questions are then: **How do you measure the impact and your value-creation?**

How do you ensure progress, and that you're doing the *right things* and doing the *things right*, when you're not counting tangible things like top-line, bottom-line, revenue, and growth? How do you gain an understanding of the intangible things that are stated in your purpose? **How do you follow-up on the triple-bottom-line?**

The answer lies in:

1. Focusing on the value you create
2. Describing its functional, emotional, and societal value
3. Aiming it at your stakeholder groups: your employees, your customers, and society
4. Establishing regular feedback loops for gathering data on the actual or perceived value, that is: **measure the impact and your value-creation**
5. Debating the mutual understanding of activities and prioritisations
6. Adjusting these activities adequately.

In other words, you apply the 'inspect and adapt' style of thinking: go and ask your customers what value they get from you. Use that as a measurement for the success and progress of your organization or team, on the same level as you measure results and revenue.

Remember that a purpose statement frames what problem you are solving, for whom, and what value you are creating.

Bain & Company described in 2015 a pyramid of value elements (appearing in Harvard Business Review in 2016 (Bain & Company 2016)), consisting of four layers of value-creation. We have converted it into a Nordic leadership style, fitted it for modern leadership philosophies, and included behaviour of multiple generations, ending with three layers of value-creation: functional, emotional, and social value-creation. Behind each layer is a number of words, each describing a value creating activity.

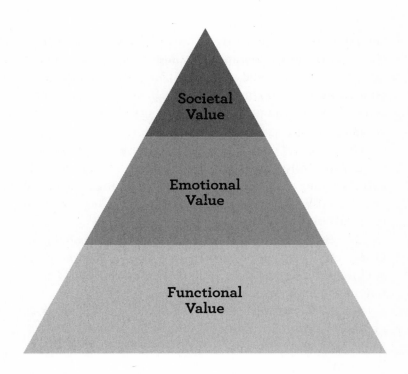

The three layers of value-creation: Functional, emotional, and social value-creation, adapted from Bain & Company

Every manager in an organization knows what functional value they create for the receiver, being an employee or the customer. However, fewer managers know or have given a thought to what emotional value they provide. And only very few managers understand what they are doing for society.

Few managers take the time to ask employees or customers how they perceive the experience of interacting with a manager or the company on each level. This is a tremendous lost opportunity for directing the energy in the organization, and understanding the effort invested in activities, projects, and products internally. Are you using your resources and time in the best possible way, and creating value for the people you're targeting your products, services, and energy towards?

The process of describing your value-creation is as follows:

Identify **who** you're providing value to. An example could be your employees, your customers, or an identified societal group. Be as specific as you can, so that you avoid generalisations, assumptions, and fluffiness.

Ask yourself what **functional** value you are creating for that person? To simplify processes? Connect things? Avoid backflow? Reduce effort? Reduce cost? Save time? Transparency? Or something else?

Next, what **emotional** value do you provide? Reduce anxiety? Clarity? Inspiration? Support? A sense of belonging? Motivation? Loyalty? Pride? Hope? Courage? Meaningfulness? Engagement? More?

And finally, what value are you providing to **society**? Do you solve one of the 17 Sustainable Development Goals as described by UN (UN 2017), or one of the 12 Global Grand Challenges, as framed by Singularity University (Singularity University 2017)?

You can capture your findings in a table like this:

Value-creation	Employees	Customers	Society
Societal			
Emotional			
Functional			

Another way of capturing the value you create is by using the Value Proposition Canvas (Strategyzer AG, The Value Proposition Canvas 2017) by Strategyzer AG, see strategyzer.com, one map for each recipient: employees, customers, and society.

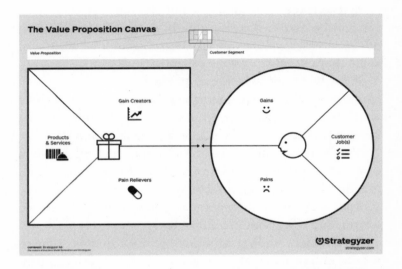

The Value Proposition Canvas, by Strategyzer AG

Measuring tangible financial or production results is done, for example, by revenue, number of transactions, time spent, or company size.

Measuring your impact and value creation is a more intangible approach, involving asking people about their expectation, experience, perception, view, and attitude towards what value you create for them.

In practise, this can be done with a weekly survey to the employees, asking them to rate the week on a 1-5 scale, or by a quarterly/half-year Net Promoter Score survey with your customers. The investigations can be augmented at times with an interview, where the employees or the customers describe the value-creation they experience or expect, using the three levels in the value-creation pyramid. This can also be used in steering committee meetings or during sales processes, where you ask your customer what kind of value they expect from your collaboration.

It can be rather awkward to ask for that kind of feedback from employees or customers the first time around. No-one wants to hear bad news or get poor ratings, but how can you know where to adjust, if you have no feedback loop?

The holistic understanding and application comes when you see the value creation in the light of the purpose, and the identity of the organization:

Your purpose statement describes what you do, for whom, and what they get out of it.

The understanding of value-creation enables you to debate and measure the impact you have on the receiver, be they employees, customers or even society.

viii.
SAY GOOD-BYE TO THE OLD
STRATEGY DOCUMENT

"Say good-bye to the old strategy document?" Well, okay, that might be a polemic, one-tonal way of stating it, and a better, more applicable phrase might be:

"Say good-bye to long-term and fixed plans, which are made and approved every three years, and only adjusted annually."

In a changing world, you cannot rest assured that a good plan with firm execution will be good for your business all the way through to the next planning event. And to be honest, I have not met any managers or C-level leaders who think so either. They all know and say that they make sure that they adapt the plan to the reality, if changes happen and if the circumstances require it.

There is, however, a disconnect between what is said, and how it is executed. Two major issues were seen at most of the companies we worked with:

Firstly, the frequency for inspection and adaption is way too low for a changing world. Annual or half-year reviews need to be replaced with monthly adjustments.

Secondly, the culture does not allow for mistakes or losing face, meaning that key stakeholders will cover up errors or be afraid to admit that they have been mistaken in either assumptions or execution.

I can recall numerous examples during my career, especially in the first decade of this century, where we were making plans for companies or large projects, where some of the most important components in the strategy were a milestone plan, a detailed description, an exhaustive stakeholder list, and a payback-time calculation. These had to be backed-up by a communication plan, describing activities and messages to be conveyed for the upcoming change and implementation, laid out for every week.

Everything had to be planned and predicted and under control, and if you hadn't thought everything through, you were subjected to a roasting from the steering committee, C-level, and the sponsors. It felt like they had made it a sport to find the holes in the presentation and material, and they had an internal battle going on to see if they could spot any weaknesses before their peer leader. They camouflaged it by saying "we're only doing this to help you", almost like a mantra.

It was not fun, and those meetings were soaked in anxiety, fear of failure, and corporate theatre. Planning was everything. Failure was devastating.

In the coming months or even years we were constantly probed and measured on our skills for planning, prediction, and control. Every proposal for change of timelines or scope was met with scrutiny and criticism, and a poorly disguised hint of failure and disappointment. Despite our aggregated learning about the product, the delivery, content, and the customer, changing the strategy and execution was tough. And the broader the anchoring in the organization, the tougher it was.

There is a clear need for a redesigned approach to strategy establishment and execution.

Instead of a waterfall-like strategy planning and execution, you need a purpose-driven intention, a clear direction and speed, a high frequency of feedback loops and opportunities for adjustment, a mechanism of collaboration across the organization, and a no-blame culture.

A wave of new mechanisms for designing and executing IT projects has rolled through IT departments over the last 20 years, and the establishment of the Agile Manifesto (Agile Alliance 2001) has launched successes like Scrum and Extreme Programming.

Some of the key design principles in these rapidly spreading and very appealing approaches and mechanisms are the tireless focus on value, the fixed-length sprints, the built-in re-prioritisation of activities, the willingness to test and experiment, and the mandatory routine evaluation of process, product, and collaboration.

In a modern workplace, the responsive leader sees the obvious combination and application of these agile mechanisms with a strategy task in a VUCA world as one of immense synergy. It allows you to maintain direction, initiate and allocate people and resources to activities based on business value, and re-prioritize with a higher frequency than before, for example monthly or quarterly.

It also ensures feedback and evaluation from internal collaboration teams, as well as from customers. In parallel, it facilitates and instils a higher degree of experimentation and innovation, which we'll also cover later in the book.

We're looking for a mechanism to establish and execute a business strategy that is both agile, and encourages innovation:

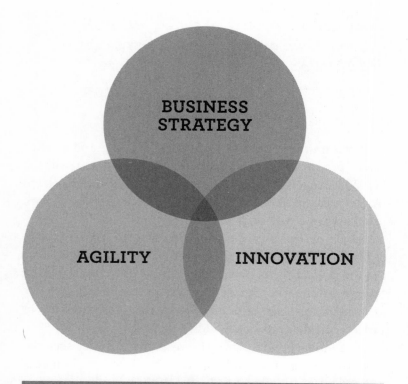

FIGURE 13

The modern organizations thrive in the intersection of business strategy, agility, and innovation

In the following description of the strategy establishment and execution, we will introduce a number of components, as replacements for the existing ones:

Old Elements	New Elements
Profit and size	Purpose and value
Analysis and deduction	Hypothesis and experiments
Functional planning	Strategic architecture
Waterfall plan	Roadmap, backlog, speedboats, and sprints

Let's look at the two phases one by one:
- Strategy establishment
- Strategy execution.

ix.
STRATEGY ESTABLISHMENT IN A CHANGING WORLD

The key component in the **strategy establishment** is the production of The Strategic Architecture, a term coined by Hamish Scott, a specialist in business strategy and former Executive Director at Ashridge Business School, London (Hamish also presented at an Open Lecture at Technical University of Denmark in 2014, and has been used by several major clients). Simplified, his approach was to ask "how do we" and "why do we" to create a **structure of shared understanding.**

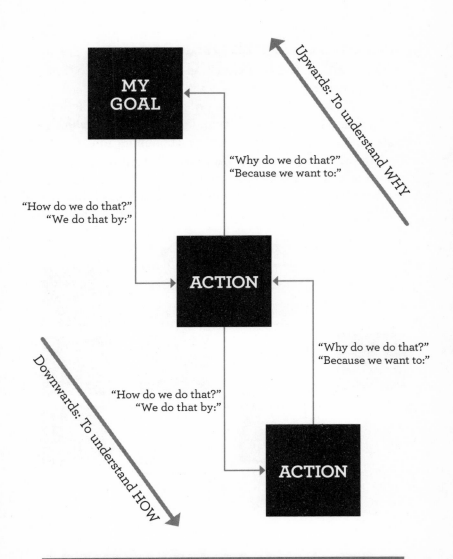

FIGURE 14

A structure of shared understanding: Downwards,
to understand HOW. Upwards, to understand WHY

The brilliance of this is that it creates a platform for reaching shared agreement and alignment. If you are in doubt about an action, you just go up a level to debate it, and regain understanding.

The approach also focuses on capabilities and actions that are detached from functional anchoring, and concentrate on shared, cross-organizational collaboration.

Finally, this allows us to keep the focus on the goal and cancel or adjust actions that are no longer beneficial to the purpose. This can happen, for example, if the feasibility of a project decreases, or if a new technology emerges.

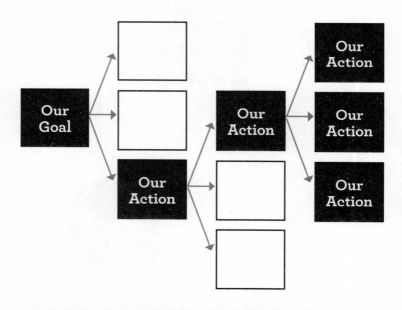

FIGURE 15

Often, this strategic architecture becomes a tree structure, with multiple shared actions supporting each other.

From here, we'll shape that a bit and combine it with Simon Sinek's Golden Circle (Sinek, Start With Why 2009), with key performance indicators (KPIs), and with Agile/Scrum to form a measurable, executable, and responsive strategy methodology that fits the modern workplace.

Scrum is a framework for managing software development. Scrum is designed for teams of three to nine developers who break their work into one-week to maximum four-week cycles, called 'sprints', check progress daily in 15-minute stand-up meetings, and deliver workable software at the end of every sprint. (Wikipedia, Scrum (software development) 2017)

For a thorough description of Agile or Scrum, please see *"Scrum: The Art of Doing Twice the Work in Half the Time"* (Sutherland 2014) and *https://www.scrum.org/.*

I've used this model in several large Danish companies, in the manufacturing, food, engineering, finance, and IT industries. Hamish Scott himself used the approach with financial services providers, leaders in the manufacturing, utility and construction sectors, media and marketing services groups, and a major airline.

The Strategic Architecture consists of three components: WHY, HOW and WHAT. Obviously, the WHY is your purpose and reason to exist. Every activity in the organization should support and enable the purpose. The WHY is our immensely ambitious goal and vision, which you must all collaborate with each other to reach. The WHY is your '20-year mission', your purpose.

The HOW is a number of non-executable organizational capabilities or mechanisms, that enables you to deliver the value requested by the customers. That might be in the form of products or services, and the value is measured not only in tangible quantities, but also in intangible qualities as described above. This is part of your KPIs, which we use to measure progress and success.

The WHAT is a number of actionable initiatives, projects, tasks etc., things that we can go and do, and then measure.

This approach can be scaled downwards to not only apply to company strategy, but also to be used for internal projects and activities. Start with the purpose of the activity, and then break it down.

A quick note on KPIs: key performance indicators are a useful way of understanding the team's progress and success, as long as they are:

- Meaningful, and enhance the behaviour and progress you want
- Based on team effort, not individual performance
- Co-created by the executing team and the reference layer (for example the product owners or top management)
- Transparent and understandable, regarding measurement method and status
- Adjusted regularly, or when they do not provide value
- Not tied into compensation or salary.

The establishment of the components in such a Strategic Architecture can be facilitated in a number of ways, for example, via a Business Model Canvas by Strategyzer AG

(Strategyzer AG, The Business Model Canvas 2017), see strategyzer.com. This will bring an understanding of the interconnection between customers, value proposition, internal key activities, and capabilities, or via a role-based archetype analysis, discovering the situation, challenge, and opportunities of the customers, employees, and other stakeholders.

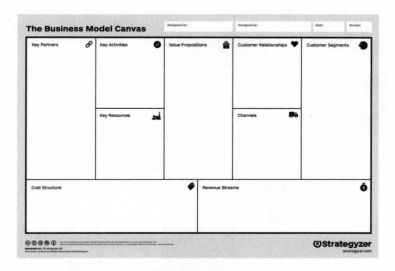

FIGURE 16

The Business Model Canvas, by Strategyzer AG

The result is a tree-structure of interconnected activities, capabilities, and mechanisms, where every element can be justified as a lever for reaching the purpose.

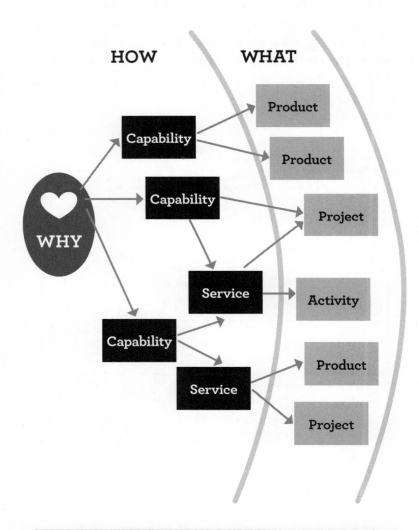

FIGURE 17

A conceptual drawing of a Strategic Architecture,
as used for example by Danske Bank

Challenging the relevance of an activity can be done by traversing upwards in the tree, until understanding and agreement can be reached. Also, if you are working on an activity or a project that cannot be mapped into the tree, you might consider cancelling it, as it does not support the purpose.

The Strategic Architecture ensures establishment of a backlog of activities, as the backlog consists of all the activities in your WHAT area. This enables you to build a roadmap with a suggestion for sequence and expected business value, and each backlog activity (each WHAT) can have its own Strategic Architecture.

An example of such a WHY/HOW/WHAT structure for an internal CRM project is:

WHY	**We** provide timely information about our current, future, and past engineering projects **So that** our sales people and marketing people **Can** use the cases for positioning, PR, and pre-sales to attract and retain the right kind of customers
HOW	Run and develop our CRM system Ensure high quality data Ensure proper usage of the CRM system
WHAT	Establish the new CRM system Move all relevant data Decommission the old CRM system Train all users Establish a maintenance team Handover to the maintenance team

X.
STRATEGY EXECUTION IN A CHANGING WORLD

What follows is the **strategy execution**, your three-month sprint (or one-month, if the cycle time allows it).

With strong inspiration from the Agile and Scrum worlds, you work your way through the activities in sprints with a length of three months, and with weekly stand-up meetings for collaboration and coordination. At all times the purpose is kept firmly in focus and as your reasoning for every activity that you choose to initiate and execute.

We will focus on how Agile and Scrum applies to the strategy discipline and to responsive leadership, specifically looking at the touchpoints between top managers and employees, and on process interfaces.

A key point here is that this Agile approach can be used and applied to strategy execution too, and not just live in the IT projects where Agile originally was born. Top management should take the Agile/Scrum facilitation and participation seriously, and handle it personally.

The design thinking is as follows:
- Strategy execution must ensure continued focus on value-creation, meaningfulness, and purpose
- Strategy execution is circular, not linear
- Strategy execution is broken into steps, to allow for feedback, feasibility evaluation, experimentation, and collaboration
- Strategy execution instils exchange of experiences, personal views, and learning.

- Strategy execution is facilitated by top management, and happens in a transparent and inclusive way

The approach is described in this process flow. Start at the top, start with the purpose (the WHY):

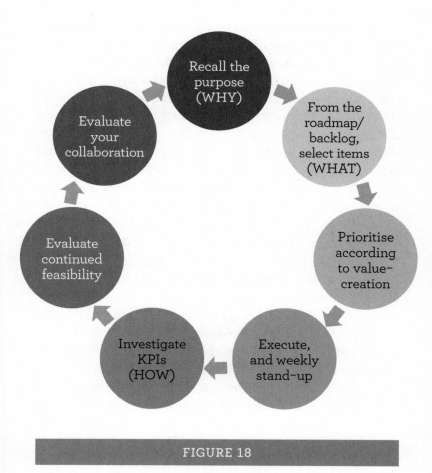

FIGURE 18

The Agile strategy execution process

In each sprint you select the activities to be executed by the organization. These activities are either existing activities that you approve for continued work, or new activities that you select and prioritize from the backlog of activities in the roadmap. You might need to investigate and test some theories by launching a 'speedboat'. See the chapter on Innovation later.

One could argue that the sprint length should be longer, e.g. six months, however, it is our experience that only very few companies are in situations where that is a feasible approach. The vast majority of organizations will benefit from monthly or quarterly sprints in their strategy execution, even if they do business in market industries where a higher degree of inertia exists (e.g. the pharmaceutical industry). The reasons are: firstly, the ability to understand and react to interdependencies in the portfolio of existing and new activities in the strategy; and secondly, the ability to investigate, test, evaluate, and embrace new emerging technologies quickly and profoundly enough.

Even when using a sprint length of one month you can – and most likely will – have strategic programmes and projects that span several sprints, maybe as long as years. The thinking behind the monthly sprints is:

- You're forced to think in, and break the work into, smaller pieces; pieces that you can handle and can have a reasonably managed approach to, with an adequate control and risk profile
- You're able to poll for feedback on the progress and value-creation of the activities in the sprint in order to evaluate the continued feasibility of the investment and, if necessary, discontinue the activity in due course
- You instil a natural habit of coordination and collaboration
- You invite and encourage experimentation.

The weekly stand-up is used for coordination and collaboration, and for sharing learning that is relevant for the other parties. This is facilitated and executed just as any other Scrum stand-up meeting would be, and it is key that this activity is handled by top management, and not delegated.

The weekly stand-up also serves as a means for communication, transparency, involvement, and interaction with those other than the traditional closed-loop/masonry of managers. Having a strategic stand-up meeting in front of a whiteboard in an open office landscape is a strong signal and message about openness, willingness to debate, desire for input, and promotion of a no-blame culture.

When employees see role models and top managers publicly discussing mistakes and failures without blaming, alienating, or pointing fingers, they see you 'walk the talk', and are motivated to copy your behaviour.

It is often argued, that 'culture eats strategy for breakfast' or some similar paraphrasing of a quote that is often attributed to Peter Drucker.

The facilitation of a weekly stand-up meeting in an open office, attended by top management, facilitated by the CEO, and with a respectful debate about collaboration, making changes, asking for help on issues, and embracing failure, is exactly the kind of culture that SUPPORTS an agile strategy.

FIGURE 19

A weekly strategy stand-up in Danske Bank,
attended by the Senior Vice President-leadership team,
facilitated by their manager, Mikko Laukka, Executive Vice
President (to the right).

The stand-up in Danske Bank took place every Tuesday
from 9am to 10am in the open office landscape. From time
to time, one or more of the employees overheard a debate,
and voluntarily jumped in to either correct a fact or an
assumption, to provide extra information for the debate, or
to be part of the decision making.

xi.
HOW TO APPLY AND ACTIVATE
THE PURPOSE IN DAILY LIFE

At the beginning of this chapter we highlighted some statements from top management, middle managers, specialists, and frontline employees, describing how they did not really understand their company's strategy and why they do what they do. This great disconnect is expressed through:
1. Lack of clear direction
2. Lack of involvement
3. Lack of meaningful goals
4. Lack of feedback loops
5. Lack of responsiveness.

Applying and activating the purpose can accommodate all of these issues and feelings, if done convincingly and with an eye for realism and stolidity in the context. Clearly, this has a strong tie and correlation to culture, and is inherently intertwined: culture is nurtured, built, and anchored most profoundly through actions, in critical processes, in pivotal decisions, and when caring for employees. Hence the need for sincerity and authenticity in the application process.

Activating the purpose has several goals, which we've seen applied in real life:

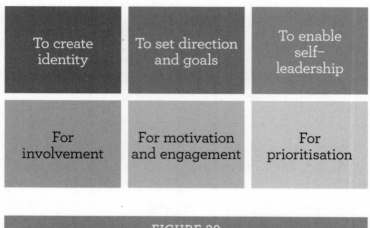

FIGURE 20

Reasons for activating and using your purpose in daily life

It's clear to see how it mitigates the 'lacks' described above, and is a means of bridging the gap; closing the great disconnect.

Mechanisms for activating the purpose are many, of which a few a listed here as inspiration.

- Present the WHY frequently, properly and convincingly. Storytelling and visuals are key to the communication, and make sure to make it personal to you. If it feels right, it is right
- Use the WHY for framing your activities, both HOW and WHAT. Put focus on what problems you are solving, for whom, and what value you create for them. The more meaning you can infuse, the better. The more relevant and genuine, the better
- Use the WHY in every presentation, at every meeting, in all discussions. Start your weekly or monthly department meeting with some examples of activities

in the past period that have helped you support and reach the purpose and goals
- Use the WHY for creating motivation and movement. Obtain feedback and statements from customers, highlighting the value you have created and the challenges or possibilities you have helped the customer with
- And most of all, use the WHY actively in decision making, when engaging people, when committing to deals, and when prioritizing tasks.

To give clear direction, make sure the strategy establishment and execution is done in full openness and with (extreme) transparency. Let everybody know what problem you're solving, for whom, and why they should care.

To enable involvement, show and tell the narrative of the purpose and the existence of the company so often and so genuinely that employees know it by heart. Make sure you involve them in decisions and prioritizations.

To establish meaningful goals, ensure that your KPIs are based on value-creation, not profit alone. Make the mechanisms of measurement, as well as the actual numbers, transparent to everybody. And, remember to debate and act on the state of the goals. *Are we there yet?* Also, setup a weekly smile-o-meter survey for employees, for example, as OfficeVibe describes (OfficeVibe 2017) or as simple as a weekly one-question survey (Bloch 2016).

To establish feedback loops, make sure you take time for weekly or monthly retrospective sessions with your employees, customers, and your peer leaders too, as part of the strategy sprints.

To establish responsiveness, plan the strategy execution in monthly sprints, ensuring feedback loops, validated learning, and a culture of ambition, engagement, no-blame, and 'it's ok to change things, if they don't work'.

xii.
SUMMARY

Having a core purpose and a clear direction is the first element in the future of work. A purpose describes what you fight for, what problem you are solving, and for whom.

You make sure to investigate the value you are creating, including the functional, emotional, personal, and societal value, and that you focus on the triple-bottom-line of the business; that is, social capital, value-creation, and economic health.

The purpose is our reason for existence, and ensures that our strategy maintains focus.

Since you are in a VUCA world, you need an agile strategy establishment and execution, which you handle by inspiration from the Agile/Scrum methodologies.

You establish a clear WHY, HOW, and WHAT via the Strategic Architecture, building a roadmap and a backlog of WHATs, and execute these WHATs in a sprint-infused manner.

Your progress is measured via KPIs and is tied directly into the value-creation you are chasing.

Finally, you make sure to establish and nurture feedback loops and involvement, both to employees and customers.

The responsive leader takes the responsibility for establishing and adjusting this mechanism.

The responsive leader also:
- Keeps bringing 'the purpose' up in conversations, in debates, and in planning sessions
- Avoids waterfall planning and execution, and favours sprints and agility over fixed schedules, even if it

requires confronting a stakeholder or sponsor with a change request

- Chases the value-creation, not only the money
- Makes sure that everyone has clear objectives, and measures them via KPIs.

ALIGNMENT WITH THE FIVE GUIDING PRINCIPLES

1. **People first**

   Ensuring that the organization has a purpose that is meaningful and motivating. Also, that you create products and projects that offer value for the customers, and make sense for the employees.

2. **Purpose, meaning, sense-making, and value-creation**

   This is the very core of it.

3. **Continuous innovation and experimentation**

   Being innovative in your approach to strategy, regarding using purpose, seeking value and meaningfulness, and regarding the tools and processes.

4. **An insatiable drive for results**

   Yes, in the sense that you're seeking and highlighting value-creation in addition to the economic health. Also, the agile method ensures frequent follow-up at the stand-up meetings, and that you do the right things in the sprints.

5. **Everybody has the opportunity to take a lead**

   Everybody is part of understanding how they create value, and how their work is meaningful and supports the purpose.

6
INNOVATION AS USUAL

The new mantra is 'challenge the status quo'. The consequence is 'continuous innovation' or 'innovation as usual'.

If you are not developing or changing your organization, you are going to be left behind.

Innovation must be an everyday thought and mindset, and used on products, processes, AND leadership.

We look at an approach for doing so, and at a model for categorizing the different classes of innovation, from everyday 'run the business' to strategic 'transform the business', but from an organizational and leadership perspective.

i.
EMBRACE AN INNOVATIVE
MINDSET FOR EVERYTHING

Innovation is a classic, highly praised, and pedestalised discipline in the business world, and a discipline that separates the crowd into two: those for whom it comes naturally, and those who see it as wizardry, science, or something of an art form that requires special skills, surroundings, and 'eureka' moments.

Those people in the latter group represent the majority of employees and managers. They are trained in doing their everyday business continuously better, focusing on doing things faster and with fewer mistakes to bring production costs down, and to increase the number of items produced. Those people might have been asked to improve their efficiency and efficacy, but they have rarely been encouraged to radically change the way they do it.

To them, innovation is something that happens in the research department, costs tons of money, and requires expensive equipment and time – lots of time. And, they think innovation requires special skills; skills that cannot be taught, especially when you're many years on from high school or university. If you don't have the skill already, you don't have a place in that world, they think.

This *innovation alienation* has no future in the modern workplace. We're living in an accelerated VUCA world, where technological achievements and sociological megatrends positively affect our ability and need for thinking differently. We need – and want – to challenge status quo, frequently.

Innovation must be part of the mindset of every employee, but we need to redefine what innovation means to employees and leaders, making it approachable in everyday activities too.

We exploit and lever the possibility of innovation in three steps:

1. Interest and thirst – The desire for innovation
2. Distribution and breadth – Innovation everywhere
3. Habits – Innovation as usual.

Innovation is not restricted to products and processes. Leadership, organizational structures, and culture must also undergo innovation and disruptive changes.

ii.
THE DESIRE FOR INNOVATION

In its essence, innovation is both desirable and necessary.

If you keep polishing and refining your products and processes without rethinking them, you end up fine-tuning and cultivating yourself out of business. This is a corollary of the 'Innovator's Dilemma' (Christensen 1997): you simply become too skilled, super-optimised, and specialized to change fast enough, when needed.

To stay in business, you need to stay relevant to the customer, and to keep up with the industry and technology. Customers are often disloyal to your products or services, and will switch to a competitor based on convenience, whether it be delivery method, technological advantages, or price. Given the advanced acceleration in technological development, the need for keeping up and staying in the loop is immense. You need to be innovative to have a place in the market.

Also, staying relevant to employees is more important than ever. Both Deloitte and Jobvite have documented this in two ways: the average tenure in a job is rapidly declining to 4.5 years (Deloitte, 2017 Deloitte Global Human Capital Trends 2017), and 18% of the workforce changes jobs every one to three years. For millennials, it is even higher, namely 42% (Jobvite 2016). Staying relevant to the courted talents or to the millennial requires three things:

1. To have the opportunity to lead
2. To be creative and have room for experimentation
3. To give guidance and have continuous conversations.

Innovation is needed and wanted, and you must embrace it more profoundly and pervasively than before. It must be on everybody's mind, all the time, to stay relevant to employees and customers. It must apply to products, processes, and leadership. It must apply to everyday actions and strategic programmes. And it must apply everywhere in the organization, in both key processes and support processes, and on every organizational level.

With that mindset:

Innovation is applying a good idea to a product or process, such that it creates value for the employees or the customers.

Innovation is the action of doing something differently, to gain an improvement.

It's not about doing the same things faster, stronger, higher, or louder, but about doing it differently, with a new tool or approach.

We can all do that. We're just not trained in it.

iii.
BE INNOVATIVE WITH
YOUR BUSINESS

It is said that "half a century ago, the life expectancy of a firm in the Fortune 500 was around 75 years. Now it's less than 15 years and declining even further." (Denning 2011)

Honestly, I don't think very many people or organizations are capable of being *disruptive*, like, *really disruptive* in the way that Google, Tesla, Netflix, Dropbox, Facebook etc. are, or were. I do, however, think that everybody and every organization can be innovative, thereby ensuring relevancy to the customer, flexibility to change when needed, and attractiveness to employees through making the workplaces cool, fun, engaging, and developing places to be.

On the other hand, disruption (also known as a disconnect, disturbance, or collapse of existing structures or technologies) scales perfectly down to each employee's work and tasks, and should be seen as something that employees can handle and embrace in their everyday life.

This requires two overall changes:

1. A mindset and culture of risk-taking and no-blame, where failure is not frowned upon. Sure, we do not want major mistakes or losses, and we mitigate that by performing small-scale tests and experiments to investigate and document the ideas and feasibility.

2. A circular approach to execution, where we work in sprints, inspired by the Agile world. Everything from company strategy to daily maintenance tasks should be thought of in circles or spirals, where we periodically stop, evaluate, re-aim, and adjust.

There is a plethora of plan-do-check-act models that applies here and, when it comes to innovation, the trick is to separate the experiments from the daily work and into its own cycle with a much faster cycle-time. The faster we can test the experiment and evaluate the hypothesis, the faster we can evaluate the feasibility. This lowers the cost of failure, and increases the speed of application.

In addition to being innovative with products, processes, and projects, you – the leader – need to be innovative with your leadership style, mechanisms, behaviour, and approach to people. Re-evaluate and reinvent your mechanisms, leadership, products and processes all the time, not just at the regular, annual 'innovation event'.

Finally, you must be innovative with your innovation.

Here we define innovation as the activity of applying a good idea to a product or process, so that it creates value for employees or for customers. Innovation is the action of doing something differently, to gain an improvement.

Innovation resides in the middle of a continuum of activities, spanning from business as usual to radical pivoting of the business:

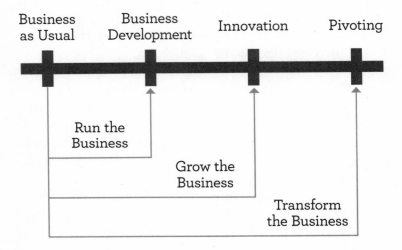

FIGURE 21

A continuum of activities, spanning from business as usual to radical pivoting of the business

The term run/grow/transform the business is coined by Gartner, and will be applied further on too.

iv.
INNOVATION EVERYWHERE

Because of the immense desire for innovation, we need to encourage and cultivate it to make it happen everywhere in the organization, and not only in special innovation labs or in the research department.

This outdated thought of 'the innovation team' or 'the innovation function' must be stamped out, and replaced with a movement and investment towards innovation everywhere, by everyone.

I've heard numerous middle managers and frontline employees complain that they do not have time to be innovative, let alone have time to evaluate and "sharpen the saw", as Stephen Covey phrases it (Covey 1989). They send clear signals that the culture of innovation is non-existent.

As with any organizational change, success relies on the behaviour of top management and the role models. You need these key influencers to put innovation on the agenda, to encourage it, to measure it, and to do it themselves. And, most of all, to accept that working with innovation will require people to do something differently than they are used to, and trained for.

This means, that:
- You must encourage employees to change things
- You must empower employees to change things
- You must embrace the fact that things change
- You must accept failure without punishment
- You must accept that innovation takes time and resources.

Encourage employees to change things

You need to state what you think is obvious: that employees are invited and encouraged to be innovative. If you don't say it and create the awareness, it will not happen. Innovation can happen everywhere, and you need to encourage employees to take on the challenge and do it.

Innovation can happen in **everyday activities**, for example, in how you conduct your meetings and create minutes, in what tool you use for surveys and data analysis, in the way you decorate your store front to be more appealing.

Innovation can happen in the **strategy establishment and execution**, for example, when entering new markets, in the partnerships, in the choice of production lines and raw material.

Introduce experimentation: **Try, Inspect, Adapt.** You can easily start with the basic 'lessons learned' approach, however that is often seen as a hygiene factor, for example, used for removing impediments and stumble stones, not for changing approaches and tools for doing something differently, to gain an improvement. The 'lessons learned' must be augmented with a 'what have we tried, what have we learned, what will we change' approach.

Here are some examples of innovation awareness activities and facilitation interventions that make people stop, think, evaluate, bring suggestions to the table, and start being innovative:

- Introduce experimentation: **Try, Inspect, Adapt**
- **Create awareness** and state clearly at every monthly department meeting that you encourage and want

everybody to be innovative and challenge status quo, both in daily tasks and also strategically
- **Infuse a 'what have we tried, inspected, and adapted' activity** into critical elements, for example, at every gate in a stage-gate model
- End **every C-level meeting** with a 'Try, inspect, adapt' session, and share the learning with everyone on the internal social media for people to comment on
- The **Retrospective** (Sutherland 2014) is a build-in activity in the Scrum methodology, where the team meets regularly at the end of a sprint to evaluate the process and the collaboration. This notion of constant encouragement to evaluate is the first step towards routinely doing things differently.

Then, based on the lessons learned, act on it. Make sure that the great ideas and innovations are applied and scaled up, and that the benefits are harvested. A tough learning from working with this is that scaling changes up is really hard, as the cost of doing so is inversely proportional to the habit of embracing changes. This also means as a corollary, that the cost of scaling up lowers dramatically as the organization gets more and more used to adapting.

Also, make innovation a HOW in your strategic architecture (see previous chapter) and focus a KPI on it. We need every leader, from top management to team leader, to ask for innovation input from their employees on a weekly basis. Let's count and measure the number and feasibility of the suggestions.

Empower employees to change things

Get everybody to think about innovation, even in the small things. Then let them actually do it. Often a good idea or a strong initiative is halted because a manager says no to change.

You can quickly kill initiative and the motivation for innovation if you say no to every idea that is proposed. This reluctance is a hindrance to growth and development, and is typically rooted in a cultural habit of control, micro-management, expectations of flawlessness, and fear of losing face.

Some companies have a pre-approval approach to any ideas that employees have, and if managers object they have to write a two-page letter of objection. Even though I like that radical idea, I see some mental obstacles for doing that. Instead, let's make a compromise, balancing empowerment, initiative, drive, practicality, and risk-taking.

I can understand that both parties in this want some kind of safety and comfort when it comes to taking chances and changing things, and a way of embracing this is to align mutual expectations to delegation, dialogue, involvement, feedback loops, and distribution of information before, during, and after the change.

Too often I have seen managers take an overly tight and controlling approach to change and to allowing employees to try new angles or tools, and the approach for getting unstuck here is to agree on the level of delegation and empowerment, and to agree on when the feedback-loops should occur.

Remember that you – the manager – always take responsibility for the actions and activities that your employees embark upon. Don't leave them to roast if they engage in new or tough things, but support them even when things go wrong. This is your duty and obligation that needs to be balanced with a sense of freedom and initiative. Yes, this is challenging to both parties.

Embrace the fact that things change

One thing I've learned from working with leaders and managers over the past decade is that change is hard, especially if the idea is not your own.

Being innovative also means breaking habits and adhering to new tools, methods, and patterns. You must leave something behind to have room for it.

This is a premise of the VUCA world, but is much harder to embrace when you're pulled into the change rather than steering it yourself.

When you ask for innovation, you get change. When you get change, change with it.

Accept failure without punishment

If employees get punished or frowned upon when they fail, you infuse fear, inertia, passivity, indifference, numbness, and apathy.

Some companies go as far as celebrating failure, installing a glass cabinet of failed products right next to the successful products, or having a 'wall of fail' next to the 'wall of fame', to send a strong signal that experiments – and hence failures – are a part of being innovative.

One great thing about agreeing on the level of delegation and empowerment, as described above, is the safety and trust it creates on both sides. We have a mutual understanding of the action we take, on the process, and on the feedback loop.

We also understand that we're trying something new, and there is inherently a chance of success, and a chance of failure. **In any case, there is 100% certainty of learning.**

This is why you should strive to obtain validated learning (Ries 2011) when you get an idea, try something different, and want to be innovative. You need validated learning to evaluate the feasibility and share the experience with your colleagues.

If you embark on an initiative that seems to have a high gearing in both success and failure, make sure firstly that you obtain learning fast, and secondly that you conduct frequent feedback-sessions with the employees.

Don't drift away from your relationships if you're trying something wild. To phrase it positively: sometimes you win, sometimes you lose, but every time you learn.

Naturally, it takes time away from productivity. It takes time and resources to stop what you're doing, allocate time to think and redesign things, and get in gear again, but you can't just allow yourself to not experiment or innovate. If you don't experiment and innovate, you'll lose customers, market share, or worse, talent.

Innovation is an investment, and should be seen as such. It's an investment in business relevancy, AND in employees. The exploration phase, the evaluation phase, and the scaling-up phase should be accounted for when allocating time and resources in your activity portfolio.

You can benefit from keeping track of it in a scheme like this:

Innovation activity	<title>
Investment in exploration	<time and resources>
Investment in evaluation	<time and resources>
Validated learning	<KPI>
Business gain	<KPI>

Even everyday innovation activities require time. Maybe it's just four hours for trying a new data wrangler tool, or fiddling with a mobile plug-in for time registration. You need to allow and encourage everybody to try new things, experiment, and learn, and you need to come to terms with the fact that it takes time away from being productive. Remember that this investment will result in valuable learning.

Finally, when evaluating the results of the innovation activity, focus on the prototypes, the demos, and the documented value-creation. Don't look at forecasts for up-scaling and for sales figures yet.

v.
INNOVATION AS A HABIT

Innovation – defined above as the action of doing something differently to gain an improvement – must be a habit and a normal thing to do. It must be an everyday way of thinking, and a close-knit mindset and mechanism.

When we look at the five guiding principles for the future of work, we can easily see that establishing innovation as a usual activity relies on cross-pollination of all the other guiding principles for the future of work:

- Innovation must bring people first
- Innovation must be meaningful, create value, and bring us closer to the purpose
- Innovation must create results
- Innovation can be led by everyone.

I've seen large companies kick-off huge innovation 'events' or competitions, where as many as 1,000 employees participated or joined in with ideas, testing, validation, and feedback. The process was well-prepared and lasted four months, from C-level kicking-off the awareness campaign, to celebrating and implementing five validated innovation initiatives.

I've seen small project teams stopping all work because a new great opportunity rose in front of them. They set aside three days to experiment and learn, wanting to find the best innovative solution to leverage the opportunity they'd found.

Both situations were built around the same process: willingness to change. Experiment. Test. Learn. Choose what to implement. Evaluate.

There is, however, a major difference in them. The company-wide innovation hackathon was initiated top-down, and driven by C-level, costing tons of time and money. The project team drove the initiative bottom-up, encouraged only by themselves, and costing only the lost production for those three days they spent on exploring the opportunity.

The cost of innovation is inversely proportional to the habitual usage; that is, the more we practice it in everyday life, the less it costs. Also, the more we are used to thinking innovatively, the more likely we are to engage in innovation activities faster. Innovation breeds innovation.

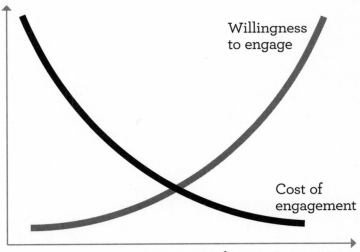

Willingness to engage

Cost of engagement

Frequency of innovation activities

FIGURE 22

How the frequency of innovation activities affects
the willingness and cost

Once we enter a state of 'innovation as usual', not only to exploit technological opportunities but to stay relevant to customers, to create value, and to pursue the purpose, several things happen in the organization. This is most profoundly seen in the employee engagement, and subsequently in the customer engagement. Both rise, and stay there.

vi.
MAPPING YOUR INNOVATION:
THE INNOVATION MATRIX

This innovation matrix characterises four areas of innovation, and innovation activities, including the leadership approach in each of them.

The model was initially proposed by Maz Spork (Spork 2017) and Søren Skov (Skov 2017), and further extended here for the leadership angles.

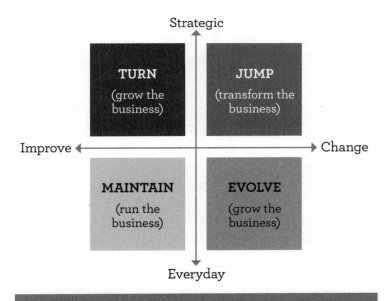

FIGURE 23

The two-dimensional innovation spectrum, from improvement to changes, and from everyday activities to strategy

131

There is a two-dimensional spectrum of situations where innovation applies, ranging (horizontally) on one dimension from mundane improvements to radical changes via exploiting disruptive possibilities, and (vertically) on the other dimension scaling from everyday maintenance to strategic pivots.

The model is annotated in two ways:

1. Using Gartner's Run/Grow/Transform methodology for describing the mindset of developing the business.
2. Describing the business mindset in said area, namely Maintain, Evolve, Turn, and Jump.

In the lower area we have everyday activities that we all take care of, as top managers, middle managers, team leads, and on the frontline.

BOTTOM-LEFT: MAINTAIN

The bottom-left area is where you typically spend most of your time, namely in 'running the business'. Here we apply innovation to 'lean and mean' the processes. This is the minimum of innovation activity you can engage in. In this area, you seek linear improvements, and this is where methods like Lean and DevOps thrive. The typical goal is 3-5% annual performance or efficiency improvements.

If you're not already doing this; that is, if you're not even performing everyday improvements, you'll be out of business very soon.

On the other hand, this is also an area where the Innovator's Dilemma exists (Christensen 1997): if you keep polishing and refining your products and processes without re-thinking, you end up cultivating yourself out of business. You simply become too skilled, super-optimised, and specialized to change fast enough, when needed. This means that you need to distribute your innovation investment to the other areas too.

BOTTOM-RIGHT: EVOLVE

The bottom-right area, 'grow the business', is where you encourage your team to exploit new opportunities. You facilitate the innovation processes and methods, you set up validated learning, and allocate time, resources, and effort to test, get feedback on, and implement the innovation.

A classical assumption is that this only happens in projects, not in operations. This is true, until you start developing and changing the way you organize tasks and teams. Once you engage in teams-of-teams and self-organizing mechanisms, and once you lower the cycle-time from development to operation, then you'll see that your team starts spending more and more time in the bottom-right area as a natural habit. Moving your focus from Maintain to Evolve requires a leadership shift, where you release control and empower the employees, and facilitate the innovation process. It is your leadership that is the key to success in this development.

TOP-LEFT: TURN

The top-left area is different, as this is where strategic improvements and innovative ideas are investigated, tested, validated, and evaluated. This is also 'grow the business', just with a higher magnitude of both gain and risk, and more focus on business feasibility than technical clarifications. This is where we 'turn the direction'.

If we were *not* to look at a revised innovation approach, this would usually happen in a strategy seminar somewhere offsite, where the top managers would plan the strategy activities based on 'things are as yesterday' thinking. They would spend time on detailed and thorough forecasting and due diligence, before investing in waterfall-planned business development activities.

However, in a VUCA world we need to be innovative all the time to accommodate and exploit the volatile, uncertain, complex, and ambiguous business landscape.

Moving from the bottom-left to the top-left is a huge challenge. The most frequently observed impediment is called 'innovators' glass-ceiling', when the corporate governance kicks in and inhibits responsiveness, agility, and flexibility. The way to change that is by embracing agile leadership on C-level. Agile leadership is inspired by the successes of Agile and Scrum in the IT domain, and several of the mechanisms can be directly applied to the C-level work:

- Having a back-log of activities
- Prioritising them in short, manageable sprints with a length of one to three months rather than yearly or half-yearly strategy reviews as we're used to
- Shared activities and goals, and KPIs focusing on value-creation
- Launching 'speedboats' to investigate and explore ideas, technology, or approaches.

This applies nicely to the innovation area, where the back-log items will be more focused on hypothesis and assumptions that we need validated learning on, for example a feasibility study on new markets, new customer segments, trends, and technologies.

The aforementioned 'speedboat' is in contrast to a 'supertanker'. A supertanker has steady pace and is hard to turn. The direction is set, the range is long, and the inertia is high. In contrast you have the speedboat: small, movable, but with short range and only a very small crew.

The analogy to organizations is immediate: The supertanker is your well-oiled production apparatus, with LEAN, with targeted organizational structures, and with a dedicated focus on the goal. The speedboat on the other hand is your experiments, explorations, and innovation projects.

These speedboats are most famous in the larger companies, but the thinking can easily be translated to your own department or the SMB's: A speedboat must have a 'quest', a crew, a time frame, a learning objective, and freedom.

The key point is speed and agility, applied to middle management and C-level. Simply put: you create a portfolio or programme of strategic activities, in which you have two or three types of sprint-cycles, in which you explore, test, validate, learn, and evaluate the opportunities. You approach the innovation with strategic and tactical initiatives with multiple speeds and cycle-times. **You go fast and slow at the same time.**

Take a quick look back to the chapter on strategy establishment and execution. You'll clearly see that these two approaches – strategy and innovation in a VUCA world – are strongly connected and can be applied simultaneously with great synergy to the benefit of the responsiveness. Also, you'll see that there is not a causality between these, but a correlation. This is exactly what we're looking for when it comes to staying relevant to employees and customers.

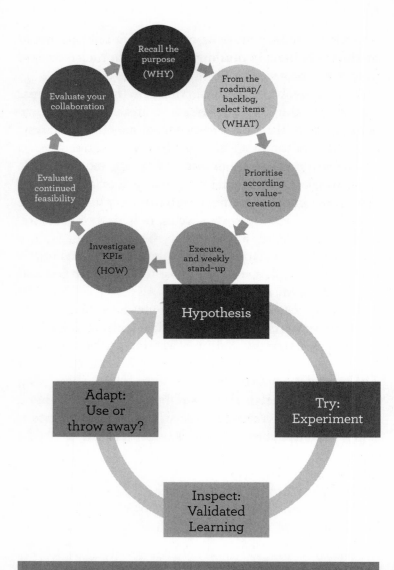

Recall the purpose (WHY)

From the roadmap/ backlog, select items (WHAT)

Evaluate your collaboration

Evaluate continued feasibility

Prioritise according to value-creation

Investigate KPIs (HOW)

Execute, and weekly stand-up

Hypothesis

Adapt: Use or throw away?

Try: Experiment

Inspect: Validated Learning

FIGURE 24

Handling hypothesis-driven experiments in your strategy execution

All this is clearly a cultural change, through a change in methodology. The leadership style is one of the responsive leader, who encourages, empowers, engages, and enables everybody to take part in the strategic activities. We are seeing a far more agile approach to strategic innovation, involving and engaging employees, key influencers, talents and leaders based on meritocracy, instead of based on titles.

- Employees are polled for input regularly (e.g. via internal social media)
- Talents and key influencers in the organization are invited and involved in the idea-generation and strategic innovation
- Middle management C-level must change their auto-response from one of risk-management, to also embrace risk-taking. This is mitigated by fast validation of the ideas and hypothesis: fail fast, fail forward, so we can learn and evaluate, and apply or throw away.

TOP-RIGHT: JUMP

The top-right area is where the business transformation is born. This is where the *really* innovative – maybe even disruptive – ideas are explored and exploited, and where the business jumps to new patterns, markets, ways-of-working, and identity and image.

The leadership style in this area is far more proactive and progressive, taking more responsibility for freedom, engagement and adaptability, with a thorough and profound focus on collaboration with the customers in new ways that maybe aren't defined yet. The leadership approach is cross-functional and diverse, based on a multifaceted view of the world. The responsive leader thrives here, and is more of a neo-generalist (Mikkelsen and Martin 2016) than a traditional leader.

Moving to this area requires a 'break-away' mindset and 'can-do' attitude. At times, teams who embark on this relocate physically to another building or part of the city to send the signal that they're doing something different than the rest of the organization. In Copenhagen, Denmark, several of these 'garage initiatives' have emerged, initiated by Danske Bank, LEO Pharma, and ISS, for example, and with huge success when it comes to creating new products, designing new processes on-the-go, and redefining cultures to match the purpose and reason for being there.

Despite the entrepreneur-like approach and the seemingly chaotic atmosphere in these teams, they are highly structured and have a strict discipline when it comes to things like regular touchpoints and feedback sessions. Facilitation and leadership play a strong role, and – as Eric Ries says in *The Lean Start-up* – the management discipline is a key element for success (Ries 2011), obtained via Agile and Scrum.

The 'let's test this, and test this fast' philosophy comes naturally in these teams, and the no-blame culture is inherent. Everything they do is focused towards helping the customers, towards solving a problem or exploiting a possibility, and towards the purpose. The work is not rooted in existing technology or business models, and there is a permeated notion of challenging status quo for the sake of helping the customers.

Teams that commit to this tend to create a culture of their own with strong connections and relationships, and might over time develop new words or phrases, or slang that is specific to the team and is part of defining them as a culture.

One concern I hear a lot is regarding the re-merge of the team and products into the existing organization; a concern I fully understand. (1) The innovation team and the organization might have two different cultures, evolved over time. (2) Those products that have emerged in 'transform-the-business' surroundings might have whole new delivery channels, form factors, support requirements, technological bearing points, and a process terminology that no-one outside the team understands. This re-merge from innovation and development back to operation must be done fast, hence the omnipresent demand of change-willingness in the organization.

vii.
LEADERSHIP STYLES IN THE INNOVATION MATRIX

As illustrated above, the leadership style differs in the four innovation areas. Here are some characteristics of the situations:

Turn
(Grow the business)
Strategic improvements

Leadership style:
Business-oriented.
Facilitating. Inviting.
Involving. Agile.

Innovation to exploit market development and ensure business feasibility.

Jump
(Transform the business)
Strategic changes

Leadership style:
Customer-oriented.
Enabling. Empowering.

Innovation to uncover serendipitous opportunities or yet-unconscious gains for the customers.

Maintain
(Run the business)
Everyday improvements

Leadership style:
Process-oriented.
Maintenance.

Innovation to create efficiency and productivity.

Evolve
(Grow the business)
Everyday changes

Leadership style:
Product-oriented.
Develop and test, based on known requirements.

Innovation to create incremental changes to the products, to exploit possibilities and technical enhancements.

The responsive leader will strive to obtain three things:

1. A shift in organizational innovation approach **away** from the default operation-oriented, linear and lean-oriented run-the-business **towards** almost anything else: everyday changes, strategic improvements, and transformational jumps

2. A culture of employees, talents, middle managers, and C-level leaders, who are courageous and committed to embracing innovation as a usual pattern of thinking and acting

3. A personal approach of situational leadership, being able to consciously and deliberately shift between the four innovation areas when needed.

In the modern workplace, the **responsive leader** empowers and enables the *employees* to manage and lead the design, execution, and maintenance of the products. The responsive leader focuses on mindset, culture, coaching and mentoring, and engagement in ongoing conversation with the employees, stakeholders, and customers.

Naturally, this happens with a situational leadership attitude (Hersey and Blanchard 1969) towards the employees and the team, depending on (a) the requirement for innovation and (b) the employee's personal needs. The responsive leader understands the situational context, the business requirements, the customers' need for value-creation, and adapts the innovation style accordingly.

The responsive leader has an insatiable drive for results, and achieves that through and with other employees. This means that they – as part of the role – act and think as an entrepreneur, working more 'on' the business than 'in' the business. A deeply rooted skill and character trait for an entrepreneur is the ability to be innovative; a natural sense for spotting new solutions to existing challenges, or cross-pollinating existing solutions to create new opportunities.

Now, these skills can be obtained by everybody! You don't need a PhD or a certain quirky personality to do it. We can all do it. However, it requires something from you and those around you: willingness and courage.

viii.
DISTRIBUTING YOUR INNOVATION INVESTMENT

A great exercise is to map all your activities into the innovation matrix, to see where they belong. You should be able to place both your **run-the-business** O&M tasks and workload, as well as every activity in the Strategic Architecture and your road-map. How many of your ongoing and planned activities are placed in the **grow-the-business** squares, both everyday and strategic? How many are placed in the **transform-the-business** square?

We will call the spread of activities in your organization across the innovation matrix your **innovation/risk-profile**. Now, ask yourself this:

Are you experimenting enough, or playing it too safe?

A safe, traditional profile looks like this – which is a profile I've met at several large organizations in the finance, pharma, logistics, IT, and energy sectors:

10%	–
70%	20%

This shows 70% of activities and allocations are spent on everyday maintenance and operations, focusing on run-the-business and on smaller, local improvements such as features and communication touchpoints. The additional 30% of the activities are used on grow-the-business, split into everyday, local change-activities and strategic improvements, which themselves are under tight governance and waterfall execution. Finally, 0% is allocated to transform-the-business.

This profile has changed rapidly and dramatically over the past ten years, and now it's not unusual to find profiles like this in both SMBs or enterprises (CEB 2017):

20%	5%
50%	25%

I have even seen this in SMBs who want to transform themselves purposefully and significantly:

30%	20%
30%	20%

They deliberately allocate a substantial amount of energy, focus, time, people, and resources to being constantly – and radically – innovative, to be relevant to their customers. Their purpose and goal is not to be innovative for the mere sake of innovation, but to serve their customers and stay attractive to the courted talent. The constant drive for learning and adapting has tremendous inertia, and is the fuel for those talents and leaders, who really make a difference, both for employees and customers. This is also where the organizations work with hackathons, so-called 'FedEx' days or 'Google time', and spend time on what seems like crazy 'under the radar' work.

The interesting part is that the more you work with this kind of innovation, the more you gain. It's a strict correlation: experimentation breeds innovation. Whoever fishes the most, catches the most. Well, up to a certain point. "Sometimes, less innovation is better," as *Harvard Business Review* phrases it (Aversa and Berinato, Sometimes, Less Innovation Is Better 2017), referring to research done by Paolo Aversa et al. (Aversa, Marino, et al. 2015). At some point, the gain from innovation will decline, namely when you work with radically new technology. Be careful when applying disruptive technology. You might end up learning that this is the wrong way after all.

ix.
BE INNOVATIVE WITH YOUR LEADERSHIP

As stated earlier in the book, in a VUCA world you have the huge possibility to be innovative with products, processes, AND with your leadership. This includes the way you think and behave, the organizational structures (see also the chapter on organizations and organizing later), and the organizational mechanisms.

The same approach for innovation that we described above applies here: **you need to experiment with your mechanisms, with your behaviour, and with your thinking.**

In general, you must consider hacking your prioritisation processes, your decision-making processes, your allocation/budgeting processes, and your collaboration processes.

An approach for this is to make a list of the leadership mechanisms you spend time on during a week. That list might contain:

- One-to-one conversations
- Performance appraisals
- Employee review and feedback
- Employee development interviews
- Project allocations
- Salary and compensation adjustments
- Talent management and development
- Hiring
- Firing
- On-boarding
- Off-boarding
- Employee wellbeing and happiness

- Stress coaching
- Organizational design
- Training and education
- Leadership coaching.

Look at the list of mechanisms in the light of the five guiding principles.

1. Do you put people first in the mechanisms, or do you perform them to comply with a business habit?
2. Do all the mechanisms create value and help you reach your purpose? Do they make sense?
3. Are you sure that your mechanisms are up to date, or even suitable for the future workplace? Are the mechanisms outdated?
4. Do the mechanisms actually provide good, useful, and timely results? And, do they ensure that your employees are on the right path for success?
5. Are the mechanisms driven by the right people? In other words, are you always the right one to be responsible for it? Maybe someone else should take a lead and handle the mechanisms instead?

As an example: given the premise that you want to eliminate hierarchies and silos, and instead be a networked organization, you should work to remove yourself from some of the hub-and-spoke processes such as one-to-one conversations and people development plans. Why not let employees help each other with development plans? They might even be better at it than you are, just because they spend more time with each other on the project teams, and therefore are in a better position to give useful and caring advice to each other.

This has been done at Pingala, a Danish IT consultancy (see the case story in chapter 12). One of the design criteria for their organization is that they want to keep the organization flat, and eliminate the need for a manager wherever possible. To do that they established an organizational network analysis (ONA) to analyse and document the real networked organization.

Based on that they constructed a chain of mentor/mentee links so that the employee development interview and sparring takes place on a peer-to-peer level in the network, and not as a hub-and-spoke structure, with the manager as the hub. The kind of new conversations that arose were fantastic, and employees got feedback and sparring from someone who had a better understanding of their professional challenges, and who they also had a social connection with. Even the CEO got an employee mentor, a reverse mentoring-approach.

x.
SUMMARY

In a VUCA world you need to stay relevant to the employees and the customers. This means that you need to be innovative all the time, with products, processes, and with your leadership.

Innovation is the action of doing something differently to gain an improvement.

Innovation must be a usual thing to embrace and engage in. Innovation alienation – the classic thinking, that innovation only happens in a special function or by specially qualified employees, must go.

Everybody must have the desire to innovate, must be encouraged to do so, and must have the mandate to change things. This then means that innovation actually happens and that things change. You, as a leader, must accept that.

Also, sometimes things go wrong. So what? Learn fast, and share the learning.

Innovation can happen to support four business scenarios:
- Maintain
- Evolve
- Turn
- Jump.

You as a manager and leader also need to be innovative with your leadership style, mechanisms, behaviour, and approach to people.

The responsive leader will strive to obtain three things:

1. A shift in organizational innovation approach away from the default operation-oriented one
2. A culture of employees who are courageous and committed to embracing innovation
3. A personal approach of situational leadership, being able to consciously and deliberately shift between the four innovation areas when needed.

The responsive leader takes the responsibility for innovation.

ALIGNMENT WITH THE FIVE GUIDING PRINCIPLES

1. **People first**
   You must create a mindset of experimentation and no-blame at the same time. It's OK to take chances and to invest time in innovation, if you ensure learning. Innovation also instils safety and trust in the future, because you keep staying relevant to the customers, hence you're also in business in the coming years.
2. **Purpose, meaning, sense-making, and value-creation**
   If you want to keep creating value and making sense, you need to be innovative. Any innovation activity is designed with the employee or the customer in mind – that is, to keep solving their problems or to exploit a new possibility. All in all, it's about supporting the purpose.
3. **Continuous innovation and experimentation**
   This is the very core of it.
4. **An insatiable drive for results**
   You, as a responsive leader, want to stay relevant to employees and to the customers, and to make results and create value. To do this in a constantly changing world, and to exploit the many opportunities,

you must engage in innovation activities. This applies to run, grow, and transform the business.
5. **Everybody has the opportunity to take a lead**
   Yes, everybody is encouraged to be innovative in their everyday business life, and in strategic changes.

7
VISCOUS CULTURE

The culture must match the mindset. We'll look at engagement, freedom at work, inclusion, empowerment, trust, and engagement.

We'll look at social capital and how to measure it via the organizational network analysis.

Finally, we'll debate the ten characteristics of organizations that have transformed into the modern leadership style.

i.
BELONGING AND IDENTITY

During my career, I've met and experienced all sorts of cultures and subcultures ranging from the highly compliant and competitive, to the inclusive and caring. The greatest cultures are the ones people are attracted to, where they like to show up to work, are sad when they quit, and return after a short period at another company. They create a sense of belonging and have constant rising engagement, and declining sick leave. An example of this is the Danish IT consultancy ProActive, described in the case study in Chapter 11.

These modern cultures are permeated by a dogmatic approach to putting people first, and yet being result-oriented at the same time.

Without a culture that fits the paradigm-shift of the future of work, you will not make it. The goal is very clear: **we need organizations where people like to show up for work**, where people will engage with each other and with the customers, and where people want to challenge the existing and contribute with input and energy. **We need organizations where people feel they belong.**

Organizational culture in the future of work is one of communities and belonging. You need to build a culture of relationships, transparency, diversity, empowerment, and trust. The personal leadership style is a key to driving and nurturing this. These communities need to be suitably viscous, in order to be both a psychological safety net and gravity point for the full-time employees, and be adaptable and inclusive for gig-workers and fluent engagements.

Martin Seligman, the godfather of positive psychology, formulated the PERMA model (Seligman 2011) for what people need in order to grow:

1. Positive emotion
2. Engagement
3. Relationships
4. Meaning
5. Accomplishments.

This applies perfectly to the organizational culture needed in the future.

Development of culture comes primarily from the behaviour of the influencers, where you as a leader have a genuine and special place as a role model. Based on the amount of followership you can establish, the ripple effect will traverse faster or slower across the organization, thereby mimicking you or totally bouncing off.

The key to developing your culture is not power, but influence, which starts with an authentic approach to the people you surround yourself with. Via networking, building relationships, giving and asking for feedback, and engaging with your employees, you begin building the foundation of a culture that is resilient, responsive, and inclusive.

ii.
A MODERN CULTURE FOR
THE FUTURE OF WORK

The challenge for building a modern culture is that the requirements for such organizations and workplaces undergo a paradigm shift and transformation. The societal megatrends and the technology advancements have changed what defines a workplace in the future. We now need to build and shape the culture to embrace new behaviour, new technology, mobility both in time and space, globalisation, and multiple, diverse generations (see for example (Deloitte, 2017 Deloitte Global Human Capital Trends 2017), (Gallup, How Millennials Want to Work and Live 2016), and (Hamel, Hackathon Report - Management Innovation eXchange 2013)). Also, the organizational culture might be physical, virtual or semi-virtual, or a mix of these over time; that is, taking advantage of digitalisation to work remotely, and use internet based tools to collaborate and communicate.

McKinsey has documented (Goran, LaBerge and Srinivasan 2017) that organizational culture is one of the main barriers to company success in the digital age. Functional and departmental silos, a fear of taking risks, and difficulty forming and acting on a single view of the customer were seen as the three main challenges for organizations.

Emergent organizations are business communities where people feel liked and trusted, are empowered and involved, and feel they belong.

These cultures follow the five guiding principles for the future of organizations:
- They put people first
- They seek purpose, meaningfulness, sense-making and value-creation
- They continuously experiment and innovate
- They have an insatiable drive for results
- Everybody has the opportunity to take a lead.

By doing so, these communities are highly adaptable to – and eager to investigate and exploit – technological changes, market demands, customer behaviour, and employee dreams.

Also, 'the way we do things around here' culture shifts from transactional or procedural, to relational. With that in mind, the culture will be an asset, and will be something that creates belonging and competitiveness. Culture is an asset, also in virtual or semi-virtual communities, and it is one you need to be almost dogmatic about.

The 'people first' guiding principle instils a culture of mutual and reciprocal engagement, safety, trust, collaboration, and care – between leader and employee, employee and employee, and leader and leader.

These cultures are characterised by an interest in each other, but also by a strong drive for production and efficiency. Relationships and results are key elements for employee happiness and wellbeing, which is reflected to the customers.

This means that the leadership must be very situational and personalised towards each employee, and the balance between the individual and the collective engagement is a constantly changing dynamic that must be catered to on a near-daily basis. The leaders in these organizations have a tremendous role in making this happen, and the behaviour is quite distinct from traditional managers. These leaders radiate "I like you. I care about you and your success. I like who you are, and what you are", and have a high level of ambition on behalf of the employees, the team, and the organization. At the same time, the leaders are ambitious and result-driven, and are fully aware of what behaviour they accept in the organization.

On the other hand, leaders who want to avoid conflicts and go too far in order to provide wellbeing will not succeed. Results will decrease, employee satisfaction will decline, and the organization will erode from the inside. I have seen that happen.

The *"Five Dysfunctions of a Team"* (Lencioni 2002) describes why this happens: the foundation for everything is trust, on which we can have a good, constructive, and respectful conflict. By basing your culture on mutual trust, respect, and transparency, and at the same time having a clear purpose with meaningful tasks, you change the conflict from 'me against you' to 'us against the problem'.

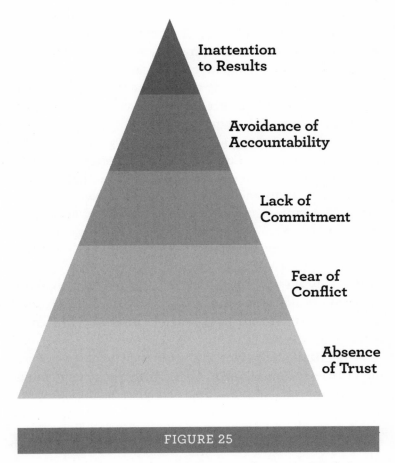

**Inattention
to Results**

**Avoidance of
Accountability**

**Lack of
Commitment**

**Fear of
Conflict**

**Absence
of Trust**

FIGURE 25

The Five Dysfunctions of a Team (Lencioni 2002).

You, as a leader, have a dilemma to handle. On one hand, you should be inclusive and involve everybody, creating a culture of democracy and freedom, embracing individual personalities, approaches, attitudes, and behaviour. On the other hand, you have the obligation to state what attitude and approach you do not want and cannot accept, both to the benefit of employees and customers, and to make sure that you create progress, results, and revenue. You do not want an employee that poisons the rest of the team or organization. You must not accept behaviour that is destructive to the culture, and you have to be consistent when it comes to addressing this.

Georg Ell, a former manager at Yammer and current Director for Western Europe at Tesla Motors, said during a CMI conference in London that companies that embark on such ambitious and weird journeys as those of Yammer and Tesla require a culture that is not fit for everybody. *"Not everyone can come on the journey,"* he said, giving examples of how strict they were when it came to taking care of the crowd of employees.

So, how do you create that kind of culture, and still maintain a balance between work and life, so that you avoid over-commitment and exhaustion, as described in *"Lethal Leadership"* (Ørsted 2013)?

Organizational culture in the future of work is a culture of business communities and belonging. You need to build a culture of collaboration. You need relationship, transparency, empowerment, and trust. You need pride, care, honesty, openness, feedback, diversity, and dialogue. And you need clear business purpose and goals.

The only thing that shapes a culture is interpersonal behaviour, so you need to build and encourage behaviour that promotes this interpersonal mindset:

- Build relationships with the employees and with customers. Get to know them on a personal level, but not necessarily on a private level
- Trust those you work with. Trust them with tasks and decisions, and with communication to stakeholders
- Empower the employees, and seek empowerment yourself.

And, most of all, you need to mix-and-dose this to every single employee. Some people hate building personal or private relationships, or really don't care about it. Some people find it vital and connect naturally to their colleagues, and are the cultural glue in the team.

No-one should be treated the same, but everybody should be addressed with the same mutual basis of respect and recognition.

iii.
GUIDING PRINCIPLES OR DOGMAS OF A CULTURE

Without doubt, the future of work is a workplace with a vision, both for the impact it has on its customers and the world, and for the kind of organization – or community – it wants to be for its employees.

It *is* difficult to describe your culture, and to put words on behaviour. But, it's worth the investment, specifically as it aligns expectations and sets guidance for the kind of behaviour you encourage, and what you disapprove of. Some organizations go farther than guiding principles, and create dogmas that are black/white in their essence.

At WD-40, they have created the Maniac Pledge (WD-40 2017), a commitment to learning:

> *"I am responsible for taking action, asking questions, getting answers, and making decisions. I won't wait for someone to tell me. If I need to know, I'm responsible for asking. I have no right to be offended that I didn't 'get this sooner'. If I'm doing something others should know about, I'm responsible for telling them."*

At Barry-Wehmiller, they agreed on *The 10 Commandments of Truly Human Leadership* (Minor and Rivkin 2016), a vision that was created by Bob Chapman:

1. Begin every day with a focus on the lives you touch
2. Know that leadership is the stewardship of the lives entrusted to you

3. Embrace leadership practices that send people home each day safe, healthy, and fulfilled
4. Align all actions to an inspirational vision of a better future
5. Trust is the foundation of all relationships; act accordingly
6. Look for goodness in people and recognize and celebrate it daily
7. Ask no more or less of anyone than you would of your own child
8. Lead with a clear sense of grounded optimism
9. Recognize and flex to the uniqueness of everyone
10. Always measure success by the way you touch the lives of people.

At Happy, they have created the *Happy Manifesto* (Stewart 2012), driven by 'Happy Henry' Stewart:
1. Trust your people
2. Make your people feel good
3. Give freedom with clear guidelines
4. Be open and transparent
5. Recruit for attitude, train for skill
6. Celebrate mistakes
7. Community: create mutual benefit
8. Love work, get a life
9. Select managers who are good at managing
10. Play to your strengths.

These three examples have a lot in common: they are based on a bold vision, they are very ambitious, they are rooted in strong human values, and they are personal.

In Pingala (see Chapter 12 for the case story), a Danish IT consultancy house, the mission is to be "an oasis for the market's most talented Dynamics 365 people for the benefit of our customers, in a lifelong cooperation." Note the order and hence the prioritisation: first and foremost, they want to build an oasis for the employees.

In Danske Bank (see Chapter 11 for the case story), a department of 120 employees have co-created a book, describing how they envision the best workplace in the world and how to get there. It contains guiding principles like:

- Tell us WHY – it has to make sense
- We care for each other
- We break down silos
- Information flows naturally and unfiltered up and down (Danske Bank 2015).

Everybody in the department participated in the work and were equally empowered, from the fresh-out-of-university junior analyst, to the Executive Vice President Mikko Laukka.

FIGURE 26

Co-creating a book on 'the perfect workplace' in Danske Bank, describing how to get there

iv.
THE TEN CHARACTERISTICS
OF THE MODERN WORKPLACE

Applying principles of a modern workplace to the organization instils a fundamental change in the way the workplace is experienced and how it shapes itself.

These are the characteristics we have identified in such organizations:

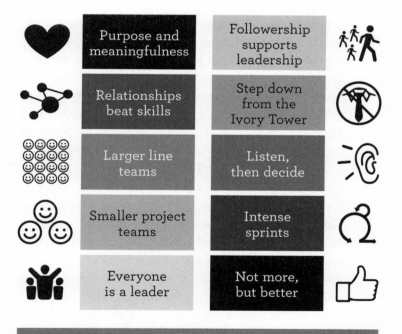

Purpose and meaningfulness	Followership supports leadership
Relationships beat skills	Step down from the Ivory Tower
Larger line teams	Listen, then decide
Smaller project teams	Intense sprints
Everyone is a leader	Not more, but better

FIGURE 27

Ten characteristics of the modern workplace

- **Purpose and meaningfulness.** The great cultures are joined together with a shared cause or belief, hence the need for a business purpose and narrative. They know what they fight for, who they serve, what problem they are solving, and what value they are creating.
- **Relationships beat skills.** Who you know and have a relationship with is more important for the productivity and getting things done, than skills. It's not that skills are unimportant. Relationships are just more important, and pave the way for the networked organization.
- **Larger line teams.** This is in direct correlation with the networked organization and the culture: the line teams grow larger and fewer, giving the leader a span-of-control that grows to double the amount from traditional hierarchical structures. This comes from a changed approach to (a) delivery structures, that are based on networked teams instead of the line organization, and (b) from the relationships between the employees, which create personal attention and a sense of belonging. This changes the role of the leader (see the description in the book).
- **Smaller project teams.** Or rather, *delivery* teams. Teams in these kinds of organizations tend to become smaller, to a size where they 'can share two pizzas over lunch', a description coined by Jeff Bezos, founder of Amazon. This both requires and nurtures a culture of relationships, trust, and transparency.
- **Everyone is a leader.** Or has the opportunity to take the lead on tasks they have the will, skill, and drive to engage in.
- **Followership** is a direct consequence of making everybody leaders: accepting that you are a follower

to the person who takes the lead on a task or activity. This action and behaviour is a huge cultural driver.

- **Listen, then decide.** The modern workplace is based on involvement and inclusion. Decisions and collaboration are based on a culture of listening to every stakeholder and employee prior to taking action. This is a tough point to implement in many organizations, where involvement and listening are a major change from the traditional power distribution.
- **Intense sprints.** Modern workplaces have a natural preference for working intensely in sprints, then stopping to evaluate, prior to engaging in yet another sprint. This stems from the ingrown focus on people and value-creation rather than technology and solution-provision.
- **Not more, but better.** The modern workplace is driven towards results and accomplishments, but not for the sake of producing many products, but rather better products. Value-creation and purposefulness is at the centre for the culture.

All this is interconnected and correlated to the culture, and will only crystallize if the culture is fit.

V.
A CULTURE OF SOCIAL CAPITAL

One of the characteristics of a modern, healthy, and responsive organization is a high degree of **social capital**, in addition to a strong focus on value-creation, technology, results and profit.

Several established philosophies and frameworks have social capital built into them. Take WorldBlu's 10 principles of organizational democracy, called 'Freedom at Work' (WorldBlu, WorldBlu 2017), *Conscious Capitalism* (Conscious Capitalism 2017), and *UNBOSS* (Kolind and Bøtter 2012). Common in each of these are networks and inclusion, interpersonal respect and freedom, and working for a meaningful purpose.

Also, look at the fantastic work done by Fredric Laloux in 'Reinventing Organizations', describing five stages of organizational evolution and the characteristics of each (Laloux 2014).

Our experience, observation, and learning from working with organizations that transform into modern, responsive workplaces is that social capital is part of the triple-bottom-line of such leaders' mindset:

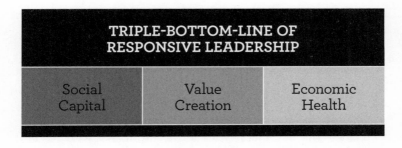

FIGURE 28

The Triple–bottom–line of responsive leadership
is nurtured by the culture

The leaders focus on these things equally, but address them in order, mentioning economic health and results last. It's well documented that organizations that focus on social capital make more money, either via higher productivity and efficiency (WorldBlu, Freedom At Work: Growth And Resilience 2015), or lower cost on employee turnover and sickness (see the ProActive case study, Chapter 11).

Social capital can and should be monitored frequently, for instance via bi-weekly ad-hoc chats, structured interviews, company surveys, a weekly smile-o-meter, or via an organizational network analysis.

The chats and interviews could use a two-by-two model like this:

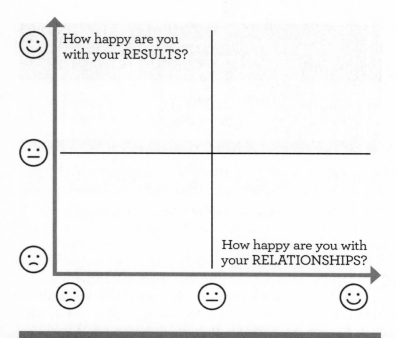

FIGURE 29

The 2-by-2 mapping of relationships and results
can help you track your social capital

This has turned out to be a good, simple framework for tracking development and seeking understanding.

Several companies have embraced the eNPS, the *employee Net Promotor Score*, as adapted from the customer NPS by Frederick F. Reichheld, Bain & Company (Reichheld 2003), asking: "On a scale from zero to ten, how likely is it you would recommend this company as a great place to work?" The point is to show that you are interested in your employees, and that you debate the score every time. Why is it high? Why is it low? What makes it change?

The organizational network analysis (ONA) provides insight into the real networks and relationships, and from that you can get an understanding of the silos, the key influencers, the kind of relationships between employees (professional or personal), and where you are vulnerable.

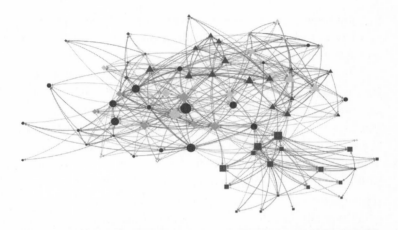

FIGURE 30

Example of a network in an organization, highlighting silos, vulnerabilities, bridgers, and key influencers

The **social capital** is both a **premise** and a **result** for modern cultures, and should be nurtured as such, feeding energy and investment into networking, relationships, and sense-making.

vi.
A CULTURE OF
DISTRIBUTED LEADERSHIP

When you want a culture that is fit for the future you need to distribute leadership and execution muscle to as many suitable employees as possible.

The thing is, you are the leader, and you have responsibility for your employees, products and services, and customers. But, you might not be the wisest, the cleverest, the most intelligent, or the most experienced in all areas. Most likely, there are employees who are better suited for specific tasks. That is a good thing, because it enables you as an organization to be more curious, initiative-oriented, creative, executing, and 'on your feet' when changes need to happen.

Distributed leadership entails three things:
1. Delegation
2. Trust
3. Empowerment.

DELEGATION

You need to delegate tasks to those who have the will, skill, ability, and drive to commit to the task. Sometimes you need to be proactive with delegation, giving responsibility for a task to an employee. Sometimes you may be more reactive, if an employee asks for responsibility of a task. In both cases, delegation and mandate are joined together, meaning you must give the employee the mandate to make decisions along with the delegation.

I have met many leaders who claim that they are good at delegating, when the truth is somewhat different due to two things:

1. They don't delegate enough. They still handle a lot of tasks and decisions that could just as well be distributed and delegated to other leaders or employees. A large study by INSEAD showed that about half of the tasks handled by leaders could and should be distributed to others (INSEAD 2014), in order to save time for the leader, and for employees to feel trusted, impactful, and important.

2. They don't delegate mandate. The employees do not feel empowered to make decisions, contact higher-ranking managers or customers, or get help and support from other employees. When you delegate, make sure that you give the employee the right mandate too. This approach requires situational leadership and a mutual agreement on what the right amount is, ranging from 'no mandate, I will decide' to 'you can decide, but you should consult me first' to 'you can fully decide'.

TRUST

Trust is something you build over a period of time. Trust can be described in many ways, of which the trust equation (Maister, Galford and Green 2000) is one:

$$\frac{\text{Credibility + Reliability + Intimacy}}{\text{Self-orientation}} = \text{Trust}$$

FIGURE 31

The trust equation

173

Credibility points backwards in time: up until now, what has someone done that makes them credible?

Reliability points forwards in time: in the near future, how do you know they can be trusted?

Intimacy is extremely situational, ranging from strictly professional, to personal, and even private on a few occasions.

Self-orientation is a killer for trust. If your colleague gets the feeling that you're doing business or collaborating with them for your own gain, the trust erodes. On the other hand, if you work together to the benefit of both of you, trust grows.

The more trust you have, the more distribution of power and mandate to a team and your employees you can establish. Mutual trust is synergetic: trust nurtures trust, and it grows slowly but steadily. Trust is built over a long period, but demolished in seconds. Managing expectations is the key here; ensure alignment to tasks, decision-making power, frequency of touchpoints, involvement, and quality.

Most of all, you should trust your peers and employees more than you, and they, are used to.

The responsive leader purposefully abstains themself from power, trusts the team and employees, and empowers them to commit themselves.

Note: There is a national-cultural dimension to this, affecting the time it takes to build trust and commit to business activities and transactions. Both Geert Hofstede et al. (Hofstede 1980) and Fons Trompenaars are great sources in this area.

EMPOWERMENT

Empowerment is a term that has been on the agenda of corporate enterprises and businesses for the past two decades; however you should see empowerment as part of a spectrum of engagement, ranging from command-and-control to commitment-and-freedom.

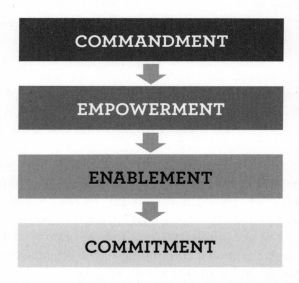

COMMANDMENT

EMPOWERMENT

ENABLEMENT

COMMITMENT

FIGURE 32

The spectrum from commandment to commitment

The thing is that empowerment has a flipside. If you're empowered to act, and the way that you handle the empowerment is not satisfactory to the one who empowers you, they can revoke the empowerment immediately. This hurts the relationship, and leaves a wound that takes a long time to heal – if it ever does.

Distributed leadership is also about creating a style of empowerment that leads to a culture of enablement; that is, employees are enabled to make decisions, they are trusted, and they have freedom to commit to tasks and transactions.

THE BENEFIT OF DISTRIBUTED LEADERSHIP

The fantastic thing is that distributed leadership nurtures freedom, motivation, and engagement.

Distributed leadership nurtures engagement at work

Power resides better in the team than in the hands of individuals. Everyone is encouraged to take a lead, drive actions and make decisions, which is a natural consequence of the drive to push the power out in the organization. You must seek advice and counselling in the organization and with the key influencers before making decisions. The larger the impact of the decision, the more advice they should seek. Power from position is shallow and short-lasting. The collective intelligence and power of the networked organization is the strongest force. You matter through people.

Also, the more organizational headroom you have for being curious, observant, and for experimenting, the stronger muscle you have for being innovative, flexible, and staying relevant to both employees and customers.

And lastly, it creates motivation and engagement. The more you delegate, trust, and empower your employees, the more engaged a workforce you get. The responsive leader should be a master in this field.

vii.
A CULTURE OF ENGAGEMENT

Naturally, the motivational basic factors have to be in place: salary, physical safety, titles, status etc., which Herzberg has described in detail (Herzberg, Mausner and Snyderman 1959).

Let's instead focus on the intrinsic motivational factors; the area where culture and leadership plays a huge factor.

Daniel Pink described in *"Drive: The surprising truth about what motivates people"* (Pink 2009) three elements for intrinsic motivation: Autonomy, mastery, and purpose.

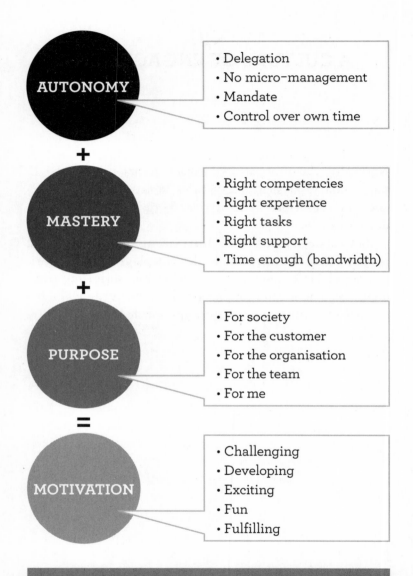

FIGURE 33

Daniel Pink's model for motivation, with details
on each component.

Based on numerous real-life experiences, interventions, and interviews, we've further codified the model to combine it with several of the new practice leadership philosophies:

Autonomy comes from delegation, lack of micro-management, mandate, and control over your own time.

Mastery comes from having the right competencies, the right experience, the right tasks, the right support from leaders and peers, and from having enough time – also denoted as having mental bandwidth to master the task.

Purpose comes on several levels, and is in line with the findings on sense-making, value-creation, and meaningfulness. It must make sense for me, for the team, for the product or services we're delivering, for the organization, for the customer, and maybe even for society and the planet.

One clear learning from the dialogues – especially when there was a deficit of motivation – was that time plays a huge factor in killing motivation. If you don't have control over your own time, you lose the autonomy. If you don't have time enough, you lose the mastery. Time was pointed out 9 of 10 times to be the single factor that creates symptoms and reactions of stress; hence, 'control over own time' and 'time enough' (bandwidth) are part of the codification.

It was, however, clear from the findings and experience that motivation is time-limited, and rarely self-contained. It needs constant nurture and focus.

Additionally, teams and organizations with a culture of **psychological safety** had highly motivated employees, which they mentioned themselves several times. This was the case in Danske Bank, Pingala, and ProActive (see the case studies), and is described and documented by Google (Rozovsky 2015): "Psychological safety was far and away the most important [dynamic for successful teams]."

A culture with psychological safety is a culture where people are engaged. This was also confirmed in our work with leaders and organizations.

A culture with psychological safety is characterised by a sincere interest in the employees' success and wellbeing.

Relationships, frequent dialogue, feedback, high ambitions, result-orientation, risk-taking, trust, and a feeling of 'I've got your back' are all part of such a culture.

Be careful not to "take your employees hostage" and expect them to be constantly motivated and engaged, which might lead to "lethal leadership" (Ørsted 2013) and mental burn-out. You have been given the privilege of being the leader for those employees for a period of their life. You must treat them with respect. The psychological safety strongly implies that the employees have the power and obligation to withdraw themselves, if needed.

Print the motivational model on a poster and put it on the wall for everybody to see. Use it when delegating tasks to see if you have the motivation for the job: is the right amount of autonomy, mastery, and purpose in place? Use it for evaluation and in your one-to-one chats. And use it to understand your own motivation and engagement.

In the long term, build a cultural understanding of the psychological safety in your team and organization. Measure it, and debate it. Trust each other.

viii.
A CULTURE OF DIFFERENT PEOPLE

There are three major reasons for ensuring, encouraging, and embracing diversity and differences in the workforce.

1. **We want to be attractive to talent.**
   A diverse workforce that candidates can picture themselves in will attract talent.
2. **We want to be responsive to changes.**
   Diversity is one of the nine design principles for adaptable organizations (Hamel, Hackathon Report – Management Innovation eXchange 2013). Diversity brings different views and angles, and has different perspectives on risks and opportunities.
3. **We want to be innovative.**
   Diversity produces creativity, which leads to innovation and competitiveness. The more diverse, the more sparks and creative ideas come forth, which leads to coming out on top and staying relevant to customers.

These three ambitions are supported by a diverse workforce, characterised by mixing male and female leadership and employees, multiple experiences and educations, multiple cultural backgrounds, and multiple generations.

Some organizations are, unfortunately, still established as 'boys' clubs'. Based on confirmation bias, men tend to hire men, making it hard to break the circle. As a leader, you must create a culture that is adaptable to both men and women, where results and actions – not words, bragging, and personal gains – are acknowledged and rewarded.

The two groups have different approaches to feedback, support, and problem solving as needed, and it takes listening skills, situational awareness, and frequent touchpoints to align expectations and to leverage the fantastic resource of diversity. It takes determination and practice.

In my experience, organizations with a more diverse workforce tend to have a more fun and vibrant mood, better discussions, a more positive outlook, and better collaboration. It does require an understanding of cultural differences, e.g. through the learning from Geert Hofstede (Hofstede 1980) or similar key resources. Your employees must understand how other cultures and nationalities perceive hierarchies, male/female values, decision making, understanding of time and deadlines, as well as humour and sarcasm. You should definitely educate yourself here.

Finally, one thing that is for sure is that we'll see a much more diverse workforce when it comes to age-related behaviour. Firstly, our working life is expected to last 60-70 years, according to Deloitte (Deloitte, 2017 Deloitte Global Human Capital Trends 2017), meaning that the Baby Boomers and Gen X/Y/Z/etc – including Millennials – will be in the workplace at the same time. Secondly, the youngest part of the workforce has grown up in a world where globalisation is advanced, and where the internet is a given (Hansen 2015). They have an innate ability to grasp the societal megatrends related to democracy and direct access to leaders, and transfer that to an eagerness for personal leadership and influence (Gallup, How Millennials Want to Work and Live 2016).

This new mixed workforce demands new behaviour, attitudes and expectations, and new work-life integration patterns. Also, it is an impatient workforce. They want to lead now (Hall 2016). They want room for creativity and experimentation. They want continuous conversation and guidance, they want a purpose, and they want to be friends with you (YoungConsult 2017). This means that the leader must handle, lead, and motivate at least two kinds of employees: those who are 'old school' and those who are 'new school':

	Traditional Workforce	New Workforce
Task Orientation	Goal oriented	Start oriented
Touchpoints With Leader	Few (less than weekly)	Many (daily)
Task Approach	Think, then act	Act, then adjust
Leadership Comes From	Skills and merits	Actions and attraction

Clearly, the diversity adds yet another dimension to the required leadership skills and behaviour: you must understand and acknowledge the differences in train of thought, age, cultural and educational background, and adapt your leadership style to the employee you're helping.

The only way you can treat people the same, is by treating them differently.

---

ix.
A CULTURE OF GIG WORKERS

One of the more recent trends in the workplace is the rise of the gig worker – also known as the freelancer – who is moving from gig to gig, from project to project, from company to company, hired in for a period of time in a temporary position.

Intuit predicts that, by 2020, 40% of the American workforce will be self-employed (Intuit 2010). This trend is expected to overflow to the rest of the world within 2025, though not with same rate. No matter what, this will definitely change the way we look at organizations, and calls for new requirements for the employees, leaders, and the cultures in the organizations.

First of all, the 'culture as a community' phrase is very real. The more the gig/freelance economy expands, the more you'll see viscous and dynamic communities emerge in your organization, where the culture is a mix of subject matter experts, business owners, delivery managers, and change-makers, all mixed between internals and externals. You'll need to get acquainted with each other very quickly, have strong guiding principles for the culture, and a clear purpose for the work to be done. It will be a culture of visual planning, dynamic stand-up meetings, and a vibrant buzz.

Secondly, full-time, permanent employees must get used to a constantly changing group of colleagues, with whom they must quickly create a connection and establish efficient collaboration. Employees must learn to on-board new gig workers and welcome them instead of feeling threatened by the externals. Gig workers should be seen as a tremendous source of knowledge and experience that you can tap into and learn from. I've heard of companies who have a rule that they want a 1:1 ratio between internals and externals, in order to create a constant flow of new input and skills, that they can learn from and be creative and innovative with.

X.
TREAT THE CULTURE
AS A PRODUCT

So, how do you build a culture that is fit for the future and for human beings?

Treat your culture as a product.

Pingala (see case study in Chapter 12) goes one step further, stating that "culture is their product", not just 'a' product.

The key to developing your culture is not power, but influence, which starts with an authentic approach to the ones you surround yourself with, namely people.

The key to developing your culture is not power, but influence.

Through networking, building relationships, giving and asking for feedback, and engaging with your employees, you begin building the foundation for a culture that is resilient, responsive, and inclusive.

However, it's not self-perpetuating or self-sustainable. It requires constant focus, drive, and nourishment.

A traditional culture is based on a product-focus with structures and titles, and is something that has a static stability to it. It does not need special attention or effort, as it is not a key lever for the productivity. **In modern workplaces, culture is built on a dynamic stability** that requires constant focus and investment, feedback and time.

Even in teams that proclaim themselves to be 'teal organizations', to use Fredric Laloux' terminology (Laloux 2014), or are on the ultimate level in self-organizing/self-managing/self-leading teams (LRN 2016) and thus have a high sense and mastery of all the mechanisms, culture requires continuous focus.

You, as a leader, play a vital role in facilitating this constant shaping of the culture, and for **addressing behaviour that is not accepted**. You must bring it up at meetings regularly, at one-to-one conversations, at strategy sessions, in the guidelines – because culture lives via behaviour, and only through the right behaviour can you get the right culture.

I have seen numerous attempts to create cultural changes, both in large enterprises and in small companies, and there is only one approach I've seen work: where they **treat the culture as a product**, and **treat cultural development as a project**. That is, to deliberately and professionally allocate time and effort to projects and activities that your employees and your customer will benefit from, and to **have someone driving it**.

Treat culture as a product.
Treat cultural development as a project.
Have someone driving it.

TEN STEPS TO TREATING THE CULTURE AS A PRODUCT:

1. Identify the purpose of the culture
2. Appoint a product owner of the culture
3. Identify what problems the culture solves, and what possibilities it creates
4. Identify what value must be created, and measure it
5. Identify key features it must have; your guiding principles or dogmas
6. Identify activities and projects that support the guiding principles
7. Make a roadmap for the culture
8. Appoint a driver or project manager
9. Address the projects on your weekly Scrum board, just as you address your other business projects
10. try, inspect, and adapt.

Remember that culture is built from behaviour, and that it's the key influencer that has the largest effect on any organizational transformation. The role models for professionalism or social capital are those that the employees look up to and mimic. The role models might be in the management team, but they are most likely also found among the regular staff. You need to find these 16% who affect the culture; those who are innovators or early adopters (Wikipedia, Diffusion of innovations 2017).

When we look at the agile production and innovation approach, and at the strategy establishment and execution, we approach the culture from a "hypothesis, build, measure, learn" stand point. We also approach it with the same professionalism and dedication as our customer-focused products. As such, remember your culture has a customer too: yourself and your employees.

xi.
HACKING YOUR CULTURE

Once you start evaluating the culture and the characteristics of it, you might come to the conclusion that improvement activities and setting focus on this-and-that might not be enough to build something that is fit for your organization, and cannot be the platform you need for the future.

Maybe you need to turn your culture in a new direction, or even transform it into something new. In both cases, you need a strategic approach and a way to break the mould.

If you look at the five guiding principles for the future of work and apply them to the current culture, you might conclude that something more transformational is required. You need less hierarchy and more networked mechanisms for decision making. You need less privacy and more transparency. You need less rigidity and more fluidity. You need a transformation. You need to hack your culture.

Hacking your culture is the action of tackling a problem from a whole new angle, breaking the existing solution into pieces, and constructing a new mechanism instead, based on the guiding principles, and on what features your culture should have [ref. the approach to culture as a product]. The key is to focus on what problem you're solving.

Such a hack requires:
- A solid foundation in your culture's guiding principles, and in your values
- A determination to change things for the better
- A willingness to invest time and effort into it

- Courage to fight for what you believe
- Patience, for when it becomes tough.

In addition, it requires willingness to let go of old habits and structures, to experiment with new things, and to dispose of that which does not work. In other words: a monstrous amount of change. This is transformational. This is responsive. This is exactly what the responsive leader does to respond to the shifts around them, both in technology and human expectations.

Some of these real-life culture hacks and case studies are:

NETWORK-BASED ONE-TO-ONES

Abolish the traditional, hierarchical hub-and-spoke one-to-ones, where the manager of a team takes turns speaking to each team member over a period of a month.

Instead, apply a **networked approach** to it and establish peer-to-peer mentoring, where the employees coach/mentor each other in small groups of three. You could use the results from an organizational network analysis to establish mentor/mentee pairs, where the mentor is a person that the mentee has referred to as a good relation, either professional or social. The third employee, a bystander, is appointed based on daily work with the mentee.

The point is to establish a culture of coaching at eye level, which is way more situational and contextual than the manager will be able to provide.

EXTREME TRANSPARENCY

Let the employees decide what you must be transparent about, and to what degree.

Make a list of everything that you can think of as information, plans, contracts, decision processes etc., and let the employees sort it in three groups: full transparency, limited transparency, and no transparency. Try to make the middle group as small as possible, and make sure to comply with the legal and HR rules also. (see the appendix for a gross list for inspiration).

Gather the list, print it, sign it, post it visibly in the office, and put it to work.

Over time you might take the list up for review. One of the most progressive companies I'm working with is putting salary on the 'full transparency' list now.

VALUE-BASED PRICING

The overall idea is that the price on the invoice is regulated by the value that you create for the customer. The higher value you create, the more money you make. This works best when you invoice the customer on a monthly basis.

When entering an agreement with the customer, you agree on what value you should deliver to the customer in addition to – or rather as a consequence of – delivering the product or service. The value can be functional (save time, simplify, make faster, connect things, integrate) or emotional (remove anxiety, create overview, provide trust).

You also agree that you evaluate the perceived value-creation every month, and that the evaluation has an effect on the hour-price this month, nudging it to +10% if more value was created, or to –10% if less value was created.

MARKET PLACE FOR CONNECTING TASKS WITH EMPLOYEES

Instead of distributing tasks to employees based on a technical or professional best fit, establish a weekly market place, where tasks are offered en-masse for employees to commit to, based on will, skill, drive, and dreams.

If it's not possible to gather the employees on a weekly basis, either due to size, location, or time, the team managers can handle this commitment on behalf of the employees. This requires that the team managers know what kind of tasks the employees dream about.

xii.
SUMMARY

A modern culture is a business community where people like to show up for work. It's a culture of engagement, freedom at work, inclusion, empowerment, trust, engagement, and of high expectations to results and getting things done.

On one hand, the culture is extremely inclusive, focusing on social capital, distributed leadership, diversity, and the fluidity of gig workers.

On the other hand, the culture is based on guiding principles or dogmas, that must be enforced in order to keep the citizens of the community close and safe: psychological safety is the difference between motivation and engagement.

The modern workplace has a triple-bottom-line based on social capital, value-creation, and economic health. The culture is a key element to reaching this.

To do so, you must approach the culture far more deliberately and purposefully. Treat the culture as a product: appoint a product owner, and drive the development with determination.

Finally, you might need to hack your culture to get where you want. A culture that is fit for humans requires some showdowns with the status quo structures and behaviour. You might need to turn the culture or jump to a total new situation or mindset.

- You must do the right things
- You must do the things right
- And you must re-evaluate what is RIGHT.

The only thing that shapes culture is behaviour. You need to change behaviour. This is hard, and this is the responsibility of the responsive leader too.

The responsive leader has one focus when it comes to culture and community: to create a sense of belonging, and a culture that is fit for employees and for the customers.

This requires a willingness to challenge the status quo and to establish some feedback loops to listen and evaluate. The responsive leader then treats the culture as a product, hacks the culture where needed, and does some experiments to see what works.

Most of all, the responsive leader establishes some guiding principles or dogmas for the culture, AND is rigorous when it comes to enforcing it: the responsive leader does not accept behaviour that is destructive to the culture. Remember, you have a responsibility for all employees, and for the business. A single poisonous employee must not shatter the culture for everybody else, or for the customers or the community.

ALIGNMENT WITH THE FIVE GUIDING PRINCIPLES

1. **People first**
   This is the very core of it. You should build an organization with a culture where people feel they belong.

2. **Purpose, meaning, sense-making, and value-creation**
   Central to the culture is the social capital and the feeling of mattering. By focusing on meaningfulness and value-creation, you embrace this.

3. **Continuous innovation and experimentation**
   Engage in experiments to develop your culture to be one where people are inspired, safe, and developed. With the new workforces entering the scene, this means that you must develop and be innovative with your organizational mechanics. Hack it, if you need to.

4. **An insatiable drive for results**

   Creating results is a factor for happiness at work, that is, for the wellbeing of your employees. It's OK, and expected from you, to have focus on results. However, results are not only financial goals, but also intangible results like value-creation, employee retention, and customer recommendations.

5. **Everybody has the opportunity to take a lead**

   This is the core of distributed leadership, and must be mixed with an understanding of situational leadership to the employee.

8
ORGANIZING FOR VALUE

Organizing is a verb, not a noun.
It's something we do – not something
we are – in order to stay relevant to both
employees and customers.

We focus on what value we deliver to the
customer, not on the product.

We look at the networked organization,
and how to transform from command-
and-control to team-of-teams.

And, we look at how this affects the
role of the manager and leader in the
line organization.

As stressed before, an accelerated world that is volatile, uncertain, complex, and ambiguous requires you to address product and service delivery from a new viewpoint.

You must look at what you do through the eyes of the customer, and specifically understand their needs and the problem you are trying to solve. This applies both to internal and external customers.

This means that your primary customer focus in the future is (1) delivering value to the customer and (2) staying relevant to the customer. This has a direct consequence on the way that you tackle product and service delivery internally, specifically how you form teams to help the customer.

In addition, the new demands from employees – especially the younger generations – puts the existing structures under stress, as adaptability, empowerment, low hierarchies, and management closeness are part of the culture and wellbeing for the employees of the future. This has a direct impact on the way that we organize our teams and delivery methods.

Less	More
Product focus	Problem solving and value-creation
Skills focus	Relationships and interactions
Hierarchy	Networks, mixed structures, and team-of-teams

i.
ORGANIZING FOR VALUE

Instead of organizing your employees merely hierarchically after functional areas or key/support processes, like research, development, production, sales, legal etc., you need to be able to organize based on the work to be done, or the value to be created.

There are two schools of thought in this field; one that focuses on fixed cross-functional teams, to which the tasks flow based on experience and best fit; and one that focuses on the tasks, and then lets people team up for the tasks based on preferences, dreams, wishes, and personal development plans.

To make this happen, the leadership role changes dramatically. Some tasks that used to be handled by the manager are now distributed to other roles inside the teams. This often comes as a challenge for existing managers.

Additionally, the management team and the collaboration within it also changes, since new methods for distribution of information, tasks, organizational energy, and employees are needed.

Deloitte have both in 2016 (Deloitte, 2016 Deloitte Global Human Capital Trends 2016) and 2017 (Deloitte, 2017 Deloitte Global Human Capital Trends 2017) documented the development in this area, giving it the descriptive name "team-of-teams", indicating the skills and dynamics needed for this to live.

This ensures self-organizing, relationship, closeness, engagement, and – most of all – adaptability and relevancy towards the customers, thereby also increasing the focus on loyalty in a changing market.

ii.
FROM HIERARCHY TO SOMETHING MORE RESPONSIVE

In the old regime, we spent time on internal structures designed after key processes and competency areas. You can easily see it by looking at classical organograms for the archetypal company, being a blue-collar or white-collar business. This is also where terms like Centre of Excellence have emerged, structures that are a celebration and greenhouse for knowledge and functional specialisation.

Typically, every three to five years in these companies you will have a re-organization, flipping the structure 90 degrees, from competency-oriented to process-oriented, or to an industry or market orientation. This makes perfect sense, since all the learning from leaning and optimising the organization, personal skills, and mastery in one dimension is carried into a new setting, in which we now invest time and effort in developing skills and mastery in the new orientation.

A new demand has arisen on top of this, which requires organizations to respond to changes and customer requests with a speed and frequency that is unprecedented.

This calls for a new way of organizing, which is driven by customer relevancy and value-creation: the **networked team-of-teams** organization. And most of all, this calls for a more fluent and self-propelled mechanism for establishing cross-functional, self-organizing (and maybe even self-managing) teams.

Sharply put, hierarchies are great for predictability and optimisation, but not so great for adaptability and innovation.

Every manager and leader I've talked with in the past decade has underlined (or claimed), that they indeed *are* capable of establishing cross-functional teams with competencies from relevant departments across the organization. There is, however, a distinct difference from company to company in how and when these cross-functional teams emerge. You should consider the following question:

Do your cross-functional teams emerge top-down, or bottom-up?

That is, are they created because the managers initiate them and ask for it, or as a natural habit and an employee-driven movement? If it's the latter, you are on the right path.

iii.
ORGANIZING FOR PREDICTABILITY AND OPTIMISATION

Hierarchies are great for producing something that needs to be the same every time, and for maximum compliance. They are great for repetitive tasks and for predictability, for example, in the production of medicine or financial compliance.

Hierarchies provide safety and comfort in steadiness and credibility, and have a clear line of command with thorough documented processes and standard operating procedures (SOPs). Some employees love this kind of organization, as it provides trust via being in control (which is not the same as controlling, however there tends to be a correlation).

Hierarchy is also a great setup for optimisation of processes, and for trimming the workforce to deliver products and services in a predictable, efficient, and effective manner. Hierarchies and 'best practices' go hand-in-hand. Lean and Kaizen are born in these structures and cultures, and work well and as intended. At times, DevOps have a great life here too, depending on the amount of continuous innovation (see Chapter 6 earlier in the book).

Hierarchy also makes it easy to plan training and education of employees, and to conduct performance appraisals, as it's clear which skills each employee needs to master; and easy to measure and evaluate how the employees and the managers fulfil their role.

Unfortunately, the hierarchies have two adverse effects:
1. Super-optimising reduces the ability to adapt. This is the 'Innovators Dilemma' (Christensen 1997) as also mentioned in Chapter 6 on innovation.

2. The management style tends towards micro-management and detailed planning and forecasting, thereby introducing a high level of governance and even red tape.

It is bad for business. If you keep optimising, polishing and refining your products and processes without rethinking, you end up cultivating yourself out of business. You simply become too skilled, super-optimised, and specialized to change fast enough, when needed. Our learning and experience from working with organizations and leaders shows that hierarchies have a strong tendency of cultivating and rewarding that behaviour.

It is bad for employees. If you keep telling people what to do, you slowly erode the capacity for creativity, and the initiative will fade away. This is often noted when the talents or the key influencers abandon ship and leave the organization for companies where they can utilise their drive and eagerness to develop themselves and nurture new thinking.

Hierarchies have immense upsides in a world where 'best practice' lives and where the business, technology, and customer expectations changes in a predictable or usual way, but not in a VUCA world.

iv.
ORGANIZING FOR ADAPTABILITY AND INNOVATION

Being able to adapt to changes that are caused by external factors like market shifts, new technology, or customer demands requires a new mindset that focuses on problem solving, not product delivery.

The big shift in how you organize is in the mindset:
you must focus on the problem you solve, not the product you deliver.

This is a dualism that you need to handle. To stay relevant to customers, you must be able to move the organization from what you can, to either what you do or what you are; or both in a fluent movement:

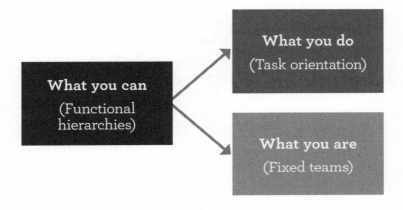

FIGURE 34

You must be able to move the organization from
what you can, to either what you do or what you are

"The Lean Start-Up" by Eric Ries (Ries 2011) underlines this demand for regrouping to deliver value to the customer, to solve the problem, to make an excellent product, and to take responsibility for helping the customer to excel in his or her situation.

The task-oriented approach requires a kind of 'market place', where employees or representatives of employees meet on a regular basis and volunteer for the tasks and projects that are up for assignment. This market place can be a physical meeting or a virtual platform, where strict discipline and interpersonal knowledge and relationship are necessary. This was the case in ProActive, where a weekly market place takes place, distributing tasks between employees, based on a deep and caring knowledge of the employees' dreams and wishes for what tasks to commit to. See the case story in Chapter 11.

Several of the Agile/Scrum coaches swear to the fixed-teams approach, where you curate employees to teams based on a set of competency and behavioural demands, including individual mastery of team roles, e.g. the Belbin team roles (Belbin 1993), or "Pioneer, Driver, Guardian, or Integrator" as Harvard Business Review presents it in recent research (Vickberg and Christfort 2017). Time is spent on building personal relationships and interpersonal skills, such that you have a fixed, well-performing team where trust is in place, and hence debate, conflicts, and disagreements are embraced and used to create even better solutions – and hence more value.

No matter which of the two approaches you embrace and experiment with, you'll need to develop several organizational skills:

- A focus on value-creation, not on products
- A focus on relationship, not only on skills
- A framework for establishing (high-performing) teams
- A mechanism for distributing tasks and projects.

And most of all, your role as manager and leader changes instantly and radically, from one of "I'm in control of the business, the delivery, the skills, and the people", to "I'm a servant of the teams, and I let them be in charge of value-creation, delivery, and applying the skills, in a situational leadership-style." We'll come back to this later.

It's worth noting that establishing this kind of team-oriented, networked organizing (which is a verb), is not a total abolishment of the hierarchy, but a redefinition of its reason to exist, the value it creates, and behaviour we experience in these structures. The hierarchies shapeshift into authorisation structures from which authority is delegated and mandated, and to guilds where employees' long-term wellbeing and development is a key area of responsibility.

The line-of-business structures will in these cases grow wider, and less deep. The management span of control will likely grow to double the amount from traditional hierarchical structures, and you will, from time to time, be able to remove a layer of managers, developing their role into something that is more oriented towards value-creation, business orientation, or customer relationship management than towards hierarchical control.

This was the case in Danske Bank. Transforming the department from silos to a more project-oriented and networked organization increased the management span, and allowed them to remove a layer of management, redesigning their role towards business relationship management and innovation instead. See Chapter 11 for a description of the case.

V.
TEAM-OF-TEAMS, AND THE NEW ROLE OF MANAGEMENT

From a theoretical point of view, you can place the organizational structures in a spectrum, from most rigid to most fluid: hierarchy, matrix (or grid or project organization), and the flat organization.

Responsive.org (Responsive.Org 2017) has identified five descriptors for organizations in this spectrum, enabling more or less predictability; or rather, less or more adaptability:

More Predictable <-> Less Predictable
Profit <-> Purpose
Hierarchies <-> Networks
Controlling <-> Empowering
Planning <-> Experimentation
Privacy <-> Transparency

Source: *Responsive.Org*

With the megatrends in society and technology, new experiments with flatter organizations have emerged, leading to an expansion of the list of structures in this spectrum to also include, for example, Holacracy (Holacracy 2017): an organizational governance with self-organizing teams illustrated as circles, and with methods for handling a number of collaboration challenges and situations like decision-making and conflict resolution.

The epiphany of new organizations and organizing is that it is highly situational, and one approach does not fit all local teams or internal demands.

Depending on the situation, the people (both employees and customers), and the value you must create, **different structures or organizational dynamics will be best fitted for each local team.**

Some might prefer a tight structure, with clear procedures and authority. Some might prefer a flat structure, driven by total flexibility. Some might prefer a fixed team. In total, this gives a mottled mix of structures that both the managers and the employees must master and thrive with.

Future organizations:
- Will organize themselves for value-creation
- Can shapeshift and respond to demands
- Will be a mottled mix of structures

Jacob Morgan calls this "Flatarchies" (Morgan, The Complete Guide To The 5 Types Of Organizational Structures For The Future Of Work 2015) as a mix of the hierarchies, the flat/networked organization, and Holacracy. This observation has been made by Deloitte too, naming it **"team-of-teams"**:

HOW THINGS *WERE*

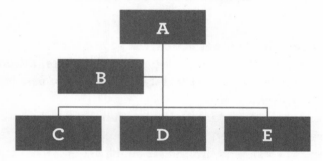

HOW THINGS *ARE*

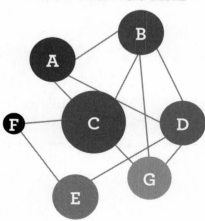

HOW THINGS *WORK*

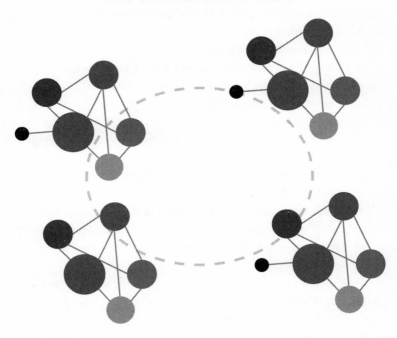

- Shared values and culture
- Transparent goals and projects
- Free flow of information and feedback
- People rewarded for their skills and abilities, not position

Deloitte University Press | dupress.deloitte.com

FIGURE 35

Deloitte illustrating the development from hierarchy to team-of-teams. Source: "Deloitte 2017 global human capital trends"

From our observations, in team-of-teams, the managers behave with some significant characteristics:

- They collaborate like a team
- They talk together, a lot
- They share information between their teams
- They share the same goal and purpose
- They take responsibility for their shared portfolio of services and activities
- They take mutual responsibility for challenges and problems
- They share resources with each other
- They coach and mentor each other
- They are indifferent to what management level they each belong to. A team can easily be constructed of managers from level 2 and level 4, for example.

As the organization evolves from hierarchy to team-of-teams or something similar, with more distributed leadership and with a multitude of local decisions on how to structure the team, the role of the management group evolves too.

A new need for distribution of information, tasks, organizational energy, and allocation of effort arises, both out in the organization, and across business units, guilds, and hierarchy layers. The communication and alignment task becomes much more difficult, as a new dimension is added to the complexity due to the abolishment of straight-forward cascading paths of instructions and information.

vi.
NEW EMERGING ROLES

This development and mottled mix of structures is a move from command-and-control, via control-of-teams, to team-of-teams.

Our observation from working with teams and leaders is that these three manager roles change in a team-of-teams structure:

1. The line manager
2. The delivery manager
3. The management team.

RELATED TO THE SUPPORT OF THE EMPLOYEE

In team-of-teams, the employee has a 'home ground' in the guild, that the line manager builds and nurtures. This is where the professional, long-term development happens, and where the employee feels at home.

The employee enters one or more delivery teams, where the delivery manager has responsibility for the employees' daily wellbeing and skill mastery. This means that there is a split in employee responsibility between the line manager and the delivery manager.

	Line Manager	Delivery Manager
Employee Feedback	Bi-weekly (macro feedback)	Daily (micro feedback)
Coaching/ mentoring	Long term, talent development (macro mentoring)	Short term, situational leadership (micro mentoring)
Employee allocation	Episode oriented, based on dialogue and the employee's wishes	Task oriented, based on dialogue and employee's will, skill, and ability

In team-of-teams, the **delivery manager** has the responsibility for delivering value to the customer in the form of a project (time limited activity), or a service delivery (in principle without time limit). This role can be played by a Scrum master, a project manager, a service delivery manager, a bid manager, a key account manager, or similar. Towards the employee, the delivery manager has the responsibility to ensure daily support and instruction regarding the tasks and the handling of those. This is highly situational, and the approach is in line with Daniel Pinks motivation theory. This we will call **micro mentoring**.

This approach affects the distribution of tasks between the employees, taking into consideration the skill, will, ability, and mutual level of trust, supported by situational leadership from the delivery manager. However, the more developed the delivery team is as a self-organized or self-managed team, the more these management mechanisms will be handled by the team members, and not as a hub-and-spoke mechanism.

Allocation to delivery projects/services is based on a mix of needs from the project and the employees' wishes, handled as a collaboration between the line manager, the delivery manager, and the employees.

The **line manager** has the responsibility for ensuring long-term talent development, which we'll call **macro mentoring**. Any dialogue here supports the employee in making their dream come true.

Based on feedback from the delivery manager – or managers, if the employee is allocated to multiple deliveries – and from the team members that the employee is working with, the line manager and the employee collaborate to grow and develop the employee.

RELATED TO THE MANAGEMENT TASKS IN GENERAL

To make the new organizational structures happen, the leadership role of the line manager changes dramatically. Some tasks that in the old workplace were handled by the line manager, are now distributed to other roles locally in the teams.

This model shows the four areas that describe the components of roles in an organization:

- The Business orientation, focusing on business understanding, vision and strategy
- The People orientation, focusing on personal and interpersonal skills and coaching
- The Delivery orientation, focusing on processes, products, and projects, and all related elements of getting things done
- The Specialist orientation, focusing on professional skills for craftsmanship, analysis, and production.

This figure is a codification of behaviour and roles that we've seen in modern organizations, and has come to be known as the 'pizza model', for obvious reasons.

Business Orientation

Business Understanding

Value chain, R&D, production, sales, marketing, internal organisation, external stakeholders and actors, compliance, market understanding, support processes, understanding the customer processes etc.

Delivery Orientation

Making Things Happen

Facilitation, project management, meeting deadlines, budgeting, analysis, estimation, building, testing, analysis, documentation etc.

People Orientation

Interpersonal Skills

Leadership, mentoring, coaching, motivation, empathy, conflict handling, emotional intelligence etc.

Specialist Orientation

Professionalism

Coding, chemistry, engineering, photography, nursery, management etc.

FIGURE 36

The so-called "pizza model" for roles in an organization

Looking at the four roles or orientations from a leadership perspective, we find that the line manager in a hierarchical organization has all four areas as their responsibility. They understand what business they're in, are responsible for delivering the products, have the necessary skills at hand (and are traditionally a master in them too), and are responsible for the employees in their business unit.

As the organizational structures evolve from hierarchy via matrix/project organization and to team-of-teams, the leadership also becomes distributed (see also section on distributed leadership elsewhere in the book). This means that the tasks and the pizza slices of the model are distributed to the team-of-teams, managed by either the delivery manager or the specialist who is the lead for the professional guild.

Traditionally, what's left for the line manager to handle is the business focus, and the interpersonal skills. This can be a challenge to some traditional managers, especially those with lots of experience in the field, and whose identity is tightly coupled with the responsibility. Those managers will have a hard time with this kind of organizing, and might take the opportunity to redesign their career and transform themselves into a specialist or delivery manager instead.

Interestingly enough, it's my observation from numerous interviews and workshops on transforming organizations and leadership roles, that an employee or manager typically prefers only two of the four pizza slices. This means that having the option to distribute the leadership tasks and consequently realigning personal preferences with the newly emerged roles is a relief to some. They are released from the tasks that they don't like or feel skilled for, and gain new traction and wellbeing in their new role.

vii.
THE LEADER'S ROLE IN
SELF-ORGANIZING TEAMS

The basic premise for engaging in new ways of organizing is to refocus the organizational energy.

Returning to the five guiding principles of future of work we see that the way groups evolve into collaborating teams is of immense importance for employees and customers:

1. People first
2. Purpose, meaning, sense-making, and value-creation
3. Continuous innovation and experimentation
4. An insatiable drive for results
5. Everybody has the opportunity to take a lead.

The point is that you, as a leader, must be able to empower the team as much as needed, enabling them to self-organize and maybe even self-manage.

You have the responsibility for supporting the team in its 'forming, storming, norming, and performing' phases (Tuckman 1965), and for paying constant attention to the dynamics from personal development, shuffling resources, and on-boarding and off-boarding employees, as each of these interruptions requires new focus on team establishment and trust.

Amy C. Edmondson (Edmondson 2012) uses a verification of team to describe what's needed: *"Teaming is something you do. It's an activity."* This fits perfectly with the premise for this chapter: organizing is something you do.

A good way of doing this is to use situational leadership (Hersey and Blanchard 1969) with the team, just as you would do with individual motivation. This team development must happen under strict and joint effort by the line managers and the management team.

The teams can evolve through several stages, touching upon aspects like self-organizing and self-management. The whole purpose of focusing on self-organizing, relationship, closeness, and engagement is to ensure employee wellbeing and engagement. This leads to adaptability and relevancy towards the customers, thereby increasing their loyalty. You play a vital role in this, ensuring that the team gets the right amount of direction, coaching, support, and delegation.

The more mature the team is, the less directive and supportive behaviour you need to apply. However, you can only stay in touch with the team members and the team development if you establish a feedback loop. That is, if you facilitate sessions of evaluation on individual and team level. This might happen on a weekly basis in the beginning, and after some months on monthly basis. Situational leadership in teams is exactly that: situational.

viii.
SUMMARY

A VUCA world makes way for new organizational structures. The hierarchies must be augmented or fully replaced with something that is far more responsive and agile, namely team-of-teams, or "flatarchies", as Jacob Morgan calls it (Morgan, The Complete Guide To The 5 Types Of Organizational Structures For The Future Of Work 2015).

We shift our mindset and approach:

Less	More
Product focus	Problem solving and value-creation
Skills focus	Relationships and interactions
Hierarchy	Networks, mixed structures, and team-of-teams

Organizing and teaming are verbs, not nouns. It's something you do – not something you are – to stay relevant to both employees and customers.

You focus on what value you deliver to the customer, not on the product.

This is a change:
- For the employee, who will experience less predicta-bility and a more dynamic workplace
- For the line manager, who must master the dynamics of teaming, of frequently matching tasks with the employees' dreams, and handle macro feedback and macro mentoring
- For the delivery manager, who gets the responsibil-ity for the micro-feedback and micro-mentoring of the employees.

My observation is, that once you start focusing on what value you deliver rather than the products you create, your leadership transformation grinds to a halt – for a short time. It hurts, and takes both convincing and experiments to get back in gear. Inspect, and adapt.

However, I've also observed, that it really pays off. The employees like it (they are happier and develop themselves more quickly than before), customers like it (they get more value, and faster), and the leaders like it (they get to work with their passion, and the peer collaboration is stronger). I've also seen this shift result in the removal of management layers, as communication, dialogue, and collaboration took place across the layers and previous silos.

The responsive leader understands that a modern organ-ization is an organization that adapts its structure and delivery mechanisms to what is needed. This demand comes both from customer expectations, and employee behaviour.

The responsive leader strives to remove hierarchies and siloes, and replaces it with a dynamic, viscous mix of locally adapted structures; that is, a mix of flat networks, of self-or-ganizing Scrum teams, and of more strict hierarchy-like groups. This changes the role of the leaders, from com-mand-and-control to empowerment and team-of-teams.

To the employees, this can be both immensely liberating, and also anxiety-provoking as the regular safe zone is replaced with something far more fluid. This requires a lot of touchpoints between the leader and the employees, regardless of whether the employee really likes this dynamic or basically refuses it. The continuous dialogue and frequent feedback loops on micro and macro level is the mitigation to this.

This will ensure that customers feel they are being taken seriously, and that the company is willing and capable of responding to new and changed requirements. If you want to stay relevant to the customer, you need to adapt.

Most of all, the responsive leader changes their mindset to one of dynamic, less predictable structures, and acknowledges that the previous competencies regarding delivery and specialist knowledge now lie in the hands of someone else (see the pizza model for reference); someone who has the skill, will, ability and drive to master and execute it way better than you are yourself.

However, the responsive leader also knows when to apply hierarchies and stringency, when needed. At times, micro-management and tight follow-up can be a source of safety and steadiness. It's all about mix-and-dose, and inspect and adapt.

ALIGNMENT WITH THE FIVE GUIDING PRINCIPLES:
1. **People first**
   The employees are assigned to activities based partly on the needs of said activities, and partly on the employees' own wishes. The wellbeing of the employees is handled on daily basis by the delivery manager, and in the longer term by the line manager.
2. **Purpose, meaning, sense-making, and value-creation**
   This is the very core of it. You organize your teams

for value-creation and problem solving, not for product focus.

3. **Continuous innovation and experimentation**
   Experimentation with the team structures and with the roles is a huge part of it.

4. **An insatiable drive for results**
   You organize for value-creation. You also support and monitor the development of the teams to become self-organizing or even self-managing. You play an important role by applying situational leadership to the teams. Results are important for the team's success.

5. **Everybody has the opportunity to take a lead**
   In a team-of-teams organization, leadership is given to whoever has the will, skill, and ability to do it. The responsive leader supports these meritocracy-based leaders with coaching and mentoring.

PART THREE:
MIX

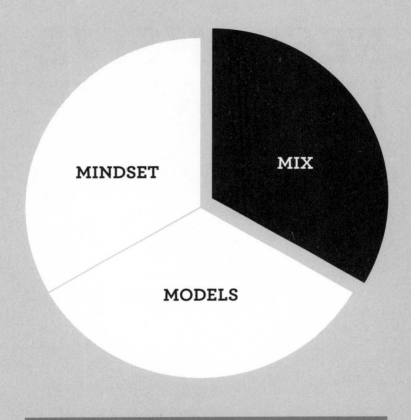

FIGURE 37

... in which we describe the role and behaviour of the respon-sive leader, the need for responsiveness, and how to mix-and-dose the philosophies and approaches when needed.

9
RESPONSIVE LEADERSHIP

Here we present the **fourth key finding: The eight key behaviours and four roles that you must master as a responsive leader.**

We describe how to apply it in your leadership style.

And we look at the traits of responsive leaders, that is, what they do to transform themselves.

Managing the five guiding principles requires a new kind of leader; a leader who is very conscious of their own behaviour and impact, and of how their role has been augmented tremendously with a new dimension of leadership: *responsiveness.*

The responsive leader both thinks and acts differently than the classical, old-workforce manager. The mindset and behaviour undergoes a paradigm shift, in alignment with the five guiding principles of the future of work, all-in-all driven and curated by the shifts in technology and society. The VUCA premise is a huge possibility for addressing work, organizations, and employees differently.

In turn, this means that the responsive leader focuses their mental energy on the moral compass, on personal development, on activating and cross-pollinating their own skills, and on understanding what is *right*:

- You need to do the **right** things
- You need to do those things **right**
- So yes, you must from time to time evaluate what is **right**, especially when you transform into a modern workplace and to being a responsible, responsive leader.

To support the process of adjusting the approach and mindset towards the future of work, the responsive leader must master new roles. Note, that this *is* a process and not something that is done overnight.

In the previous chapters, we've shown how this paradigm shift impacts the four business elements: purpose and direction, innovation, culture, and organizing. Now we look at how this affects and changes the role and behaviour of a leader.

Both during my own development as a leader and by observing and supporting business leaders in Denmark, it seems clear that the responsive leader is focused on people, is a great and frequent communicator, is determined, makes fast decisions, handles risk via experimentation, and thrives with adapting to new situations, new people, new technology, and regulations. They are also emotionally intelligent, and build trust by opening themselves and revealing some of their personality.

Our observations show that responsiveness, agility, and adaption is a key skill to resilience – both as a company and an individual – and it all starts with the mindset; a mindset anchored in the five principles of future of work, and grounded in an understanding of the development in technology and society.

However, the responsiveness must be counterbalanced by suitable inertia and viscosity. The eagerness for adjusting and adaption must not end in 'flutter' and lack of direction. This balance is learned after a period of time, working deliberately with the transformation to a modern, responsive leader.

Our learning is that it takes 3-6 months to change your centre of gravity to the new philosophy and mindset, but 12-24 months to master the balance.

i.
YOUR ROLES AS A LEADER

As seen in the previous chapters, working with purpose and direction, innovation, culture, and organization in the modern workplace requires the responsive leader to take on and assume a role with four specific elements to it. This role is based on people skills, business drive, a holistic understanding of the dynamics within the organization, and social capital.

The responsive leader is:
- A coach and a mentor
- An entrepreneur
- A master of 'white space'
- A gardener of the ecosystem.

These elements are in alignment with the five guiding principles of the future of work:
1. People first
2. Purpose, meaning, sense-making, and value-creation
3. Continuous innovation and experimentation
4. An insatiable drive for results
5. Everybody has the opportunity to take a lead.

Let's go through them one by one.

COACH AND MENTOR

ENTREPRENEUR

MASTER OF WHITE SPACE

GARDENER OF THE ECOSYSTEM

FIGURE 38

The four roles as a responsive leader

You must master both coaching and mentoring, and apply it with situational leadership both towards the individual employees and towards the team as an entity.

Google Inc. has 'be a good coach' as the top of their *'Eight qualities of a great manager'* (Google 2017). Of those eight, only the last one is about technical skills; the rest is about people.

The responsive leader cares about the development and wellbeing of the employees and of the team, and invests time in helping each employee be successful, and be the best version of themselves. This means frequent conversations and sparring, open questions, and at times also hints, direction, and advice. As coach and mentor, the leader creates trust, safety, and confidentiality, and is ambitious on behalf of the employee.

As **coach**, the leader is a facilitator for drive, ideas, understanding, and reflection. A coach asks questions and guides the employee to seek answers themselves.

As **mentor**, the leader also has attitude, opinion, multiple views, and experience, and will voice it. A mentor comes with specific suggestions to the challenges the employee is experiencing.

Additionally, sometimes you also must be an oracle, and should prescribe a solution or approach. The delicate challenge lies in balancing these three: the coach, the mentor, and the oracle.

A key to being a good coach and mentor is mastering emotional intelligence (EQ), namely the ability to identify and handle your own and other people's feelings (Wikipedia, Emotional intelligence 2017). It's all about your empathy and sympathy, and about striving to understand both your mentee, and yourself. You'll have an easier time helping other people if you understand yourself.

In 2017, More Than Sound, LLC (Goleman and Boyatzis 2017) created a breakdown of the domains and competences of EQ, which you can use as a tool for self-assessment and for working with your mentees' emotions:

- Self-awareness
  - › Emotional self-awareness
- Self-management
  - › Emotional self-control

- › Adaptability
- › Achievement orientation
- › Positive outlook
- Social awareness
  - › Empathy
  - › Organizational awareness
- Relationship management
  - › Influence
  - › Coach and mentor
  - › Conflict management
  - › Teamwork
  - › Inspirational leadership

Dave Gray at xplane.com has published (D. Gray 2017) a great way to map your understanding of your employee, customer or partner, in a way that ties nicely into the Business Model Canvas (Strategyzer AG, The Business Model Canvas 2017) and Value Proposition Canvas (Strategyzer AG, The Value Proposition Canvas 2017).

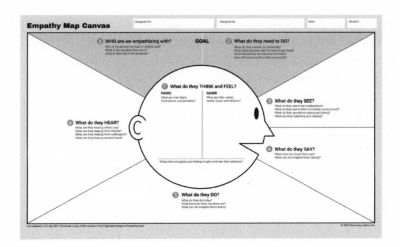

FIGURE 39

The Empathy Map Canvas by Dave Gray, xplane.com

You must **think and act as an entrepreneur,** and see yourself as CEO of your team or department.

The entrepreneurs or scale-up CEOs I've been working with or coached have all had a balanced approach to working ON or IN the business. An entrepreneur is used to switching between working ON the business (with the purpose, direction, positioning, market understanding, PR, marketing, networking, research, sales strategies, ensuring pipeline etc.), and working IN the business (selling, developing, producing, delivering, running projects, handling service etc.).

This approach and way of thinking can be directly transferred to the role of a leader, and with a tight connection to situational leadership on the team. Think and act as an entrepreneur, focusing also on the exterior context of your team:

- How does the (internal) market look? Who in your organization wants your product, and what problem are you solving?
- Who should you work with to be successful? Who are your partners and your suppliers?
- What value are you creating for your customers, and for your customers' customers? How do you measure that, and bring it back to your Product Owners and team?

The most successful business unit managers or department leads I've met are the ones that also act like business relationship managers or key account managers, focusing on the dynamics between the delivering team and the receiving team.

This has also been observed by several professional product owners and product managers; they increasingly act like mini-CEOs, with a holistic yet collaborative view on their market space (Ernst 2017).

It is important to underline that how to apply the entrepreneurial role is tightly connected to the state and maturity of your team and department. Low maturity regarding team development means that you should focus your energy inwards. The more self-organization and self-leadership in the team, the more you should focus your entrepreneurial energy outwards.

You must **master white space management:** management of the area between the boxes in an organizational chart.

The great department leads or team leads that I've met have also had a good understanding of the things that 'fall between the boxes'; that is, the decisions that have no owner, the product requests that no-one has discovered or exploited, scope that no-one has thought of, initiatives that are not harvested, or 'skunk work' that is not used.

White space management is a concept described by Rummler and Brache in 1991 (Rummler and Brache 1990) as the area between the boxes in an organizational chart, where very often no one is in charge. This also is where "rules are vague, authority is fuzzy, budgets are non-existent, and strategy is unclear" (Minzberg, et al. 1988).

Those responsive leaders who master white space are those that see the blind spots of the organization, and strive to close the gap by investigating, analysing, suggesting an approach, and facilitating a decision on it.

A key competence to do this is a holistic mindset and understanding of the internal organization and the dynamics of execution. Also, being able to predict behaviour of the internal stakeholders and knowing their strengths helps the white space manager to find and uncover issues and possibilities.

A way to approach and accommodate this is to seek dialogue and information-sharing frequently. You should strive to understand patterns of behaviour and thought, and strengths of the managers and key influencers in the organization. The goal is to jointly create a full picture of the situation, and to find the things that fall between the cracks, together.

You must be a **gardener of the ecosystem** around you.

Lastly, you have an important role when it comes to managing collaboration between all the leaders and key influencers, especially horizontally in the organization. You must be a **gardener of the ecosystem** around you, such that the dynamics of a strengths-based leadership team is nurtured, and that dialogue, engagement, and access to expertise are facilitated. This is one of the aspects of the so-called social business, namely facilitation of the health of the leadership ecosystem between the leaders.

Compared to 'leading downwards' to your teams and 'leading upwards' to your leader, 'leading horizontally' is many-fold tougher and a neglected or ignored discipline, especially in organizations who have not transformed away from hierarchies.

One traditional impediment for this is performance management. If you're being monitored on local products and KPIs, you really must break this pattern and deliberately invest extra time in collaborating with your peer leaders, getting to know them, helping them with resources, and asking them for help. You must do this, even though you know that it takes focus away from their inherently incentive-directed behaviour.

The times I've seen this occur in companies, something special happens with the holistic, internal-shared understanding of togetherness, solidarity, and culture. When you bypass, or supplement the hierarchy with mechanisms of cross-organizational collaboration on leadership level, your employees feel it immediately, and it frees time and energy for the managers that you report to. In return, this gives you even more space and empowerment to thrive in. It's a positive spiral.

ii.
YOUR BEHAVIOUR AS A LEADER

By observing, interviewing, and analysing the development and results of hundreds of leaders, I've tried to codify the behaviour and skills that responsive leadership requires.

If you have read the previous parts of the book, this listing cannot come as a surprise, as they capture the means of establishing the strategy, the innovative production, the culture, and the suitable organizations, based on the five guiding principles of the future of work. **Thus, these eight elements are at the core of the behaviour:**

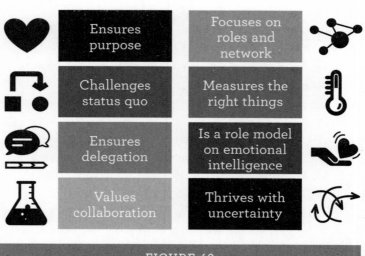

FIGURE 40

The eight behaviours of a responsive leader

- **Ensure purpose and meaning**
  The responsive leader establishes the WHY, and ensures that they are making a difference. They understand what problem they are solving, or what possibility they are creating. They strive to create meaningfulness in every action and task. They must be an excellent communicator and speak vividly about their vision for the future – and be an even better listener. A great pep talk includes three key elements: direction-giving, empathy, and meaning-making (McGinn 2017).

- **Challenges the status quo**
  The responsive leader challenges the way things are done, both HOW and WHAT, and for products, processes, and leadership/organizational mechanisms. Also, they encourage the team to do the same. The responsive leader knows that they are not always the wisest, the brightest, the most experienced, nor the one with the best ideas – hence they invite the employees to challenge the way things are done.

- **Ensures dialogue and delegation**
  Direction and traction is made through intense dialogue, and from delegation of tasks and mandate to those who have will, skill, and drive for it. Transparency, trust, and autonomy are key elements for doing this, which is a self-perpetuating premise for successful empowerment.

- **Focuses on collaboration, innovation, and experiments**
  The responsive leader values collaboration, innovation, brainstorming, and experimentation to strive for new ideas, everyday improvements, and strategic changes. A key skill is facilitation of team work and collaboration, including encouraging team members

to try new stuff in controlled experiments, focusing on testing the hypotheses and creating validated learning. If we cannot predict the future (remember, we're in a VUCA world), we can establish some tests to confirm or reject ideas fast, with as little effort and investment as possible.

- **Focuses on roles and network**
  It's documented by MIT and DTU jointly that teams created based on relationships outperform teams that are created based on skills (de Montjoye, et al. 2014). The responsive leader focuses on what you can make happen rather than what title you have. This kind of followership and network is both a competitive advantage in the market, and something that the younger generations (Millennials, Gen Y, and Gen Z) look for and appreciate in organizational cultures, ((Hall 2016), (Hansen 2015), (YoungConsult 2017), (Hamel, Hackathon Report – Management Innovation eXchange 2013), and (Deloitte, 2017 Deloitte Global Human Capital Trends 2017)).

- **Measures the right things**
  As described earlier, the modern bottom-line is a triple-bottom-line, consisting of social capital, value-creation, and economic health. The traditional stakeholder-centric financial maximization is replaced by a company-centric orientation, focusing equally on relationship, meaningfulness, value-creation, customer satisfaction, and economic health. This means, that the traditional KPIs will be augmented with, for example, organizational network analysis (ONA), employee happiness and satisfaction, and customer net promotor scores (NPS), to monitor the social capital and the value-creation. The responsive leader ensures that you get weekly data on this, it

is presented and debated transparently in public, and that actions are taken. Without feedback loops like this, you cannot act and respond suitably agilely.

- **Is a role model on emotional intelligence**
The responsive leader is authentic, present, intimate, and personal; all without being private and awkward. They are emotionally intelligent; that is, capable of identifying and handling their own and other's feelings. They see the best in people and allow them to take initiative, take chances, make mistakes, learn, and grow. The responsive leader creates psychological safety, while still being ambitious and insatiable for results.

- **Thrives with uncertainty**
The responsive leader must thrive with the uncertainty of the future, knowing that micromanagement, privacy, and closed-loop decisions are the wrong reaction to your own anxiety. Instead, they tackle uncertainty by (1) openly sharing thoughts, (2) experimenting with new things to dismantle risk, and (3) listening to others' learning. By constantly being curious and courageous, a lot of the uncertainty can be turned into a dynamic energy of creativity.

Three things are very important when it comes to the skills and behaviour of the responsive leader in this light:

1. No-one can master all eight of these skills. The best and most adaptable leaders that I've worked with have mastered five or six of them, and assembled a team around them to jointly cover all eight fully. However, within the skills they master, they do it to the max.

2. Each of these skills must be applied with situational leadership into the context of the organization, employees, and culture. The responsive leader manages this without losing the personal anchor and core.

3. You must still be a great manager to be a great leader. The classic virtues of managing scope, time, cost, quality, risks, and resources are still needed, and are a foundation for being a leader on top of this.

In all the cases in this book there are leaders who master this. They are great examples of curiosity, courage, willingness to take chances and to experiment, and sensitivity towards feedback and learning. Most of all, they have an irresistible drive towards success through, and with, people. They all act out their leadership in accordance with the five guiding principles of the future of work.

iii.
APPLYING RESPONSIVENESS

The responsive leader takes a holistic view on work, and understands that they must work actively with all five parts of the model at once, as the elements are correlated and affect each other.

The practical approach to this is described in the previous chapters, covering strategy, purpose and direction, production and innovation as usual, viscous and engaging culture, and how to organize the workforce for value-creation.

Working with the five areas of Future of
Work requires responsiveness

One of the absolute cardinal characteristics
of the responsive leader is responsiveness.

One of the primary skills for organizations and for leaders is to master the right amount of responsiveness. Meaning that you must adapt and adjust your leadership style and approach, responding on **micro level** to the situation, the challenge, and the team, and on **macro level** to the shifts in technology and society.

Sometimes you need to be tight and instructing, creating an organization that is efficient and predictable.

Sometimes you need to be empowering and supporting, creating an organization that is responsive and less predictable.

Both profiles are useful, but you need to know:
1. When to choose what profile or 'setting'
2. How to shift between them
3. Which elements affect each other.

The responsive leader has a 1-to-5 balance between the old-school and the new-school leadership styles.

To build on Jacob Morgan's image of the experiential organization (Morgan, The Employee Experience Advantage 2017): you need to know when to be in the factory, and when to be in the lab.

To do so, the responsive leader takes on a proactive 'inspect and adapt' role, having eyes and ears towards a vast and exhaustive number of touchpoints, opinion makers, influencers, demands, and possibilities. These include the employees' individual needs and development, the team dynamic, the internal market and stakeholders, the external market, the customers, the community, the technology, the industry trends, and society.

The only way to tackle this is by proactively testing, probing, and experimenting with the options, and then to respond to the feedback, fast.

The responsive leader combines the five guiding principles with the five areas of the future of work with an 'inspect and adapt' approach to 'mix-and-dose' the old, traditional management style with the new-practice leadership.

FIGURE 42

Combine 'Inspect and adapt' with 'mix-and-dose' to get the responsive leadership

This requires an experimental and innovative approach to strategy, delivery, culture, and organizing, all rooted firmly in a mindset of empowerment, engagement, and trust.

iv.
TRAITS OF A LEADER IN TRANSFORMATION

The strongest and most successful new practice leaders I've met in the past decade have all mastered the ability to 'mix-and-dose' the leadership style, according to their short-term development and to their long-term transformation. They shift their centre of gravity to the new practice leadership, but know when to be controlling and demanding, either to ensure culture, progress, or to deliver value.

I have learned that those leaders who undergo transformation and embrace the paradigm shift quickly and smoothly, possess these five traits:

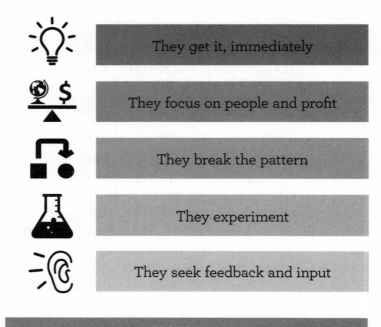

FIGURE 43

The five traits of a transformative leader

THEY GET IT IMMEDIATELY

They immediately 'get it' and have a natural tendency to thrive with it. It's like turning on the lights in a room they are already in, or cleaning their glasses.

To them, speaking of future of work and the modern workplace comes naturally. They are already aware of technological and societal trends, and are curious, eternal learners. Their leadership style makes room for new abilities, and amplifies the existing, but untrained skills.

They typically have an 'epiphany moment' that they can remember clearly, and once they have experienced the work-life of a responsive leader – and seen the responses in the employees and stakeholders – they want to continue the journey.

THEY FOCUS ON PEOPLE, PLANET, AND PROFIT

They focus on purpose, meaningfulness, and value-creation, as well as results and profit. They are fully aligned with the triple-bottom-line of the modern workplace: social capital, value-creation, and economic health.

They go to work to create more than just profit, and do not care about being the strongest in their industry, but focus on how they can create value for the receiver, i.e. for their colleagues, for the team, for the customer, for the customer's customer, or for the planet.

Results and profit still have a professional, strong position, but are outweighed (but never outshone), by the quest for meaning and purpose.

THEY BREAK THE PATTERN

Entering the world of the modern workplace requires a lot of patterns to be broken.

The successful transformation starts when the leader understands the need to replace the existing mindset with a new one, and that it involves breaking a lot of systems, habits, and behavioural patterns.

The transformative leader focuses on a vast number of things at once, all at the same time. They understand that they cannot change just one thing at a time. They need to work with all the elements, simultaneously: purpose, innovation, culture, organization, and leadership.

THEY EXPERIMENT

They experiment, and try new approaches to feedback, one-to-one conversations, project methodologies, visual planning, remote work, IT tools etc.

I've seen leaders experiment with network-based mentoring, visual strategy planning, stand-up meetings on top-level, speed-feedback, 24-hour sprints, hackathons ... followed by evaluation and adjusting.

In particular, I've seen transformative leaders experiment with their own role, trying to actively remove themselves from the epicentre of power, making space for the team members and their leadership.

THEY ACTIVELY SEEK FEEDBACK AND INPUT

They seek feedback often, and use it openly and transparently for improving the culture, wellbeing, and behaviour.

Also, the transformative leader constantly listens to input from inspirational sources, reads articles, listens to podcasts, and in general stays alert and hungry.

V.
SUMMARY

The final of the five elements in the future of work is responsive leadership. This leadership requires that you take on four new roles:

COACH AND MENTOR

ENTREPRENEUR

MASTER OF WHITE SPACE

GARDENER OF THE ECOSYSTEM

FIGURE 44

The four roles of responsive leadership

The roles are brought into practice via eight specific behaviours, that you must master:

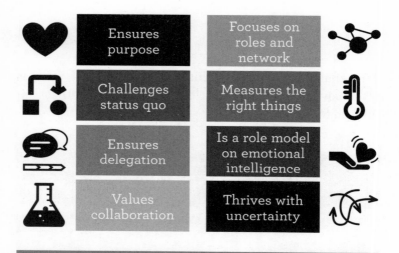

FIGURE 45

The eight behaviours of responsive leadership

Finally, and most significant for the responsive leader:

You must know when to mix-and-dose the old and the new style.

The process is rewarding. The results are substantial and measurable, and have been documented thoroughly, also in the case studies of Danske Bank (Chapter 11), Pingala (Chapter 12), and ProActive (Chapter 11). Examples are:

- Significant increase in ratings in employee evaluations
- Continuous increase in weekly happiness-measures
- Employees nominate their leader in a competition for Best Young Business Leader
- Continuous decreasing sick leave
- Significantly more network relationships established both in the team and across the teams.

The critical move is to take the *leap of faith* and have the courage to get started.

Five guiding principles

1. People first
2. Purpose, meaning, sense-making, and value-creation
3. Continuous innovation and experimentation
4. An insatiable drive for results
5. Everybody has the opportunity to take a lead

Triple-bottom-line of responsive leadership

Social Capital	Value Creation	Economic Health

FIGURE 46

The full codification of the responsive leadership,
and the correlation between the models

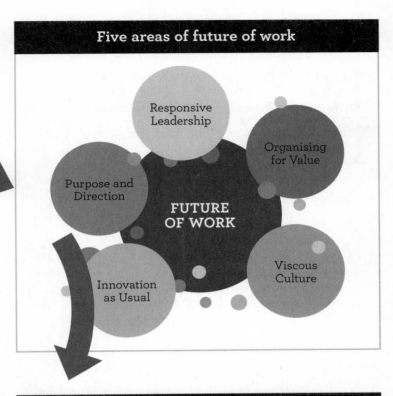

Five areas of future of work

Responsive Leadership

Organising for Value

Purpose and Direction

FUTURE OF WORK

Viscous Culture

Innovation as Usual

Roles and behaviour of the responsive leader

Coach and mentor	Ensures purpose	Focuses on roles and network
Entrepreneur	Challenges status quo	Measures the right things
Master of white space	Ensures delegation	Is a role model on emotional intelligence
Gardener of the ecosystem	Values collaboration	Thrives with uncertainty

10
TAKE THE TWO STEPS

One of the frequently asked questions related to leadership development is, "How do I start?"

The answer is, "Take the leap of faith and have the courage to get started. If you want to, you can do it."

It's important to understand that the leader of the future focuses on all five of these elements *at the same time*:

FIGURE 47

The five areas of the Future of Work

These five areas are correlated. You cannot work with just one or a few of the elements, and expect the transformation to happen. You need to embrace all of them. You can start with a little piece of each area, but your philosophy, mentality, mindset, and approach to tasks, challenges, development, and people, must contain all five areas. When you adjust one area, it influences the other four in a correlation you'll understand when experimenting and observing. Inspect, and adapt.

Does that mean that you're all good if you understand the five guiding principles, and embrace the five elements in the future of work? Well, yes, sort of.

It is the **first step** in the big shift: shift your centre of gravity to this new practice of leadership. Have the willingness and determination to do something different, and to try it out.

Understand why the world is changing. Understand the design principles of the future of work, and apply it to the five elements of the future of work, when you transform and develop your new style. Combining these two will create the responsive leadership, but only if you apply it using feasibility thinking, in your organization and situation. This operational application is highly contextual, and the activities you need to execute cannot be given fully in this book.

The **second step** is just as important, namely the actual transformation into a responsive leader of the future. This happens when the behaviour becomes a habit.

The responsive leader has shifted their centre of gravity, but knows when and how to deviate from the new style, and mix, match, and dose it with selected mechanisms and elements from the old, traditional, more hierarchical and predictable style. This requires an experimental and innovative hypothesis-based approach to strategy, organizing, and execution, all rooted firmly in a culture of empowerment, engagement, no-blame, and trust.

Transforming uncritically to the new style – without situational awareness for dosage in the spectrum of application – will result in mistakes, and has the risk of breaking your team or your management group in two parts. You might even end up disappointing yourself and your employees. Clearly, you need a focus towards the new centre of gravity, but a healthy mix-and-dose is the only sane way to get your team, organization, and peer leaders with you.

However, this must not be an excuse for falling back to the old leadership style, or for not engaging fully in it. Yes, there is an entry barrier in transforming, and you need to pass that. It takes persistence and determination, but the result is rewarding.

Some good advice for getting started:

Tell your employees and management peers that you're doing something new. Tell them what it's about, and what inspires you to do it.

Let your employees and management peers know that you will most definitely make some mistakes in the next 6–12 months, and that you are eager to listen to their feedback.

Work in sprints, just like you would with your business. Stop, and evaluate monthly.

Team up with another leadership colleague in your organization. It is much easier to grow when you do it together.

11
CASE STUDY: DANSKE BANK

– A TRANSFORMATION OF A DEPARTMENT

COMPANY CHARACTERISTICS

Company Name	Danske Bank
Industry	Financial services and banking
Company Size	Approx. 19,000 employees
Global Presence	Danish headquarters. Offices in several other countries
Employees in the Case Study	Approx. 120 employees in the Risk Analytics department, with 18 nationalities, spread across several locations in Denmark, and with a department in Vilnius, Lithuania

In February 2015, the Executive Vice President of Risk Analytics at Danske Bank, Mikko Laukka, announced to the whole department that he wanted to initiate a rather substantial culture and collaboration project, affecting all 120 employees in Risk Analytics.

The idea and the subsequent business case was formulated in the six months prior to the announcement in February, based firstly on the observation and understanding of new technologies entering the financial services market in general and the banking industry specifically, and secondly on higher expectations from customers with regards to internet banking, automation, self-service, and personalisation.

Danske Bank has, for a long time, kept a keen eye on the development of technology and society. To the bank's managers and employees, VUCA meant a lot of uncertainty and volatility, especially from the new players in the Fintech-market. Danske Bank has seen this as both a challenge and an opportunity, and has, over the years, initiated several innovation and culture projects with success across the organization, also initiated from the CEO. MobilePay is one such example.

The management team around Mikko Laukka – his own manager, his peers, and his direct reports – understood this VUCA world and what challenges it posed. Laukka seized the inherent opportunity and ran with it, in alignment with other similar transformational movements in the bank. Instead of staring blindly at the obstacles, Laukka and his team made a list of what they knew, both regarding the market and the expectations from the employees.

Laukka states: *"We know what we need to deliver:*
- *Automation*
- *Accurate, transparent decision support*
- *Simple and efficient credit platform*
- *Model framework with correct risk ranking*
- *Portfolio Risk Management.*

We know what we must improve on:
- *Collaboration*
- *Agility."*

Instead of solely initiating a product-driven portfolio of activities aiming at delivering automated financial services, Laukka and his management team directed their focus and energy into the employees and the culture first and foremost; a design-thinking that is fully in line with the first of the five guiding principles of the future of work, namely 'people first'.

Laukka explains: *"We focus on development environment, behaviour and agility, in two waves:*

Wave 1
- *Kill the silos within Risk Analytics*
- *Exceed all expectations as top place for employee development*
- *Dare to step outside the box*
- *Keep expertise, add sales and service mindset*
- *Deliver consistently on a high level – day to day.*

Wave 2
- *Kill the silo of Risk Analytics*
- *Build on created trust across organization*
- *Provide the analytical expertise across the Group."*

With that, Mikko Laukka and the management team in Risk Analytics initiated a substantial project on culture and delivery, wanting to transform the department into a modern workplace with less hierarchy and more agile delivery methods. Mikko Laukka wanted to build the best possible workplace. Little did he know that the experiences and learnings they were embarking upon would end up covering all five of the guiding principles of the future of work:

1. People first
2. Purpose, meaning, sense-making, and value-creation
3. Continuous innovation and experimentation
4. An insatiable drive for results
5. Everybody has the opportunity to take a lead.

APPROACH

From that point on, an enduring, tough, but fruitful teamwork was initiated. Over the next few months, the management team and the organization together designed and conducted several activities. Five major elements were the bearing points of 2015:

1. The formulation of the business case – or rather, the business justification of the activities. Laukka and the management team wanted to create a modern workplace where people wanted to show up every day; a workplace that was without unnecessary hierarchy, and that focused on empowerment, collaboration, and agility; a workplace where people could thrive and grow. As an indication of this development, the employees' happiness was measured weekly via a smile-o-meter, used for debate about wellbeing both on a department level and in the local teams.

2. Grand meetings in February and March, kicking off the transformation for all affected employees. Here the awareness of, and desire for, the transformation was initiated, and the messages highlighted and stressed by the key influencers in the department, not just by the management team.

3. An Organizational Network Analysis, documenting that the silos were indeed not only rumours or perceptions, but very much fact. This analysis was rerun every 9-12 months to document the development of the network and the cross-team collaboration, and to monitor the erosion of the silos.

4. A portfolio of activities, executed via a tightly facilitated and monitored agile process with clearly defined inspect-and-adapt mechanisms. Every Tuesday morning at 9am the management team had their weekly, stand-up meeting to support each other in the cultural projects and activities. This created a shared understanding of the power of collaboration, transparency, and honest debate, and served as an example to the rest of the department. Also, every second week, everyone in the department was invited to a 30-minute stand-up meeting where

they went through the status of all activities and projects, transparently. The first two or three meetings
were rather 'polite' and almost all KPIs were in green,
but as the employees saw and felt that they were safe
and that actions were taken accordingly, more honest reporting and requests for help emerged. Yes, the
KPIs turned to yellow and red, but the transparency
and frequent touchpoints created a rippling understanding and togetherness.

5. A huge workshop for every employee in June, where
the whole department co-created a culture book,
answering two questions. Firstly, what does the
world's best workplace look like, and secondly, how
do we get there? This resulted in two things: a shared
vision and picture of where the department was
heading, and a long list of suggestions for activities
to engage in. This also gave a clear indication of what
kind of leadership was needed for the employees:
empowerment, delegation, a more fluid form for
organization, and acknowledgement of employees'
work and contribution.

Mikko Laukka's deeply rooted intention was to create the
best workplace possible, a dream that required the drive and
ambassadorship of both his management team and the key
influencers, without whom the transformation never would
have taken place. The management team played a huge role
in this, being role models and operational front-runners of
new behaviour and mechanisms.

To get the vision in place for all employees, they formulated the purpose of the department, striving to make
sure that every action within the department supported
this purpose: "Creating the analytics-driven banking of
the future."

This was used to describe what the vision meant to society, to employees, to partners, and to shareholders, to understand what value the department should create for these roles. Laukka presented the purpose and the related activities that supported getting there with the words: "If your project or activity is not on this chart, then it's because you work on something that is wrong and we should stop it." That made a huge impact on the understanding of meaningfulness in tasks over the following years.

To support the drive for collaboration, agility, empowerment, and team-of-teams, Laukka and the management team initiated a programme of training activities and delivery mechanisms, inspired by the Agile movement and Scrum. Everybody was trained in Agile Project Management, and the product owner role was introduced in parallel with the establishment of a project management office.

In line with the understanding of empowerment and the notion of 'everybody has the opportunity to take a lead', the product owner role was often placed with a local product expert, and not by reflex with a manager. This helped to support the movement for empowerment, meritocracy, and involvement. The managers and team leaders played a huge role in constantly focusing on self-managing teams, striving to establish the network-of-teams thinking and structure.

For the managers, this meant rather substantial changes to their roles. Every manager was trained in modern leadership to give them an aligned mindset and skillset, preparing them for a redesign of the role of the line manager: less focus on delivery and skills, more focus on coaching, building and maintaining relationships, and on helping the employees in prioritising their work and energy.

Finally, as part of the organizational change management – and to listen to the employees – a reference group was established, consisting of a representative from each team, but without participation from the management team. This served as a safe place to air frustration in an anonymous way. Over the course of the two years, the topics covered substantial elements like employee trust, anxiety, and identity, as well as operational elements like physical surroundings, tone-of-voice in communication, and compensation; all equally relevant and important for motivation and engagement in a department that is redefining several crucial components, in parallel with running the daily business of a bank.

RESULTS AND LEARNING

It was not without obstacles and challenges. People (both managers and employees), got frustrated, anxious, and made mistakes, which was anticipated from looking at the J-curve of change management. As expected, and as noted in the initial business case documentation, not all employees wanted to be part of the journey. During the first six months, the turnover rate of employees doubled but, interestingly, the empty spaces were quickly filled as the idea of the culture spread and became apparent in mindset and behaviour. Because these employees wanted to stay within the culture, they did not leave the department at the usual rate.

In the autumn of 2015, Laukka and the team re-ran the Organizational Network Analysis and documented that the silos were indeed cracking, and communication in the department was, to a larger extent, networked, not cascaded. Ergo, the network collaboration and communication was growing, and the team-of-teams approach was winning ground. This made it possible to have larger line teams.

This led to the bold but natural move of eliminating a management layer, introducing the concept of networked leadership, and redefining the role of the line manager to be focused more on employee mentoring and goals, than on product delivery and product ownership. This meant that the management team grew from four to eight direct reports to Laukka.

This also led to a higher manager-to-employee ratio of 1:12, with some managers having up to 25 reports at times. To handle the relevant 1-to-1 dialogue with the employees, a new mechanism of peer-coaching and peer-onboarding was initiated.

2016 was spent in a slower gear, focusing on letting the changes sink in, on performing a few experiments on mechanisms regarding peer-coaching and personal development plans, and on rerunning two major components; namely co-creating the culture book, and performing the organizational network analysis.

Clearly the change had been tough and demanding on both employees and managers, which was a useful – but not surprising – learning. It was very important to invite and involve everybody to engage and participate, without which the transformation would not have taken place.

WHAT NOW?

The transformation was a success. Employees developed the habit of seeking purpose, empowerment, and low hierarchy, and were disappointed when they collaborated with employees outside the department and observed that the same mindset was not in place everywhere.

Mikko Laukka, being the observant and ambitious leader he is, did not settle for mediocracy, but kept asking himself questions like: "Are we getting complacent? Do we need to do something differently? Or more? Or less?"

Laukka saw the need for continuous re-enforcement of the mindset and the mechanisms, for two reasons. Firstly, over time such a radical idea and transformation fades gradually and is caught up in daily work and routines. Secondly, as new people enter the organization, they need to be trained in the updated mindset, which at the same time is a clear opportunity to remind everyone about the journey they have embarked on.

Laukka and the management team wanted to create the perfect workplace. "Not good, or better than average, but perfect," he wrote in the preface of the second cultural book of the department.

They have come a long way already – but they are not done yet.

12
CASE STUDY: PINGALA
– WHEN CULTURE IS YOUR PRODUCT

COMPANY CHARACTERISTICS

Company Name	Pingala A/S
Industry	IT consultancy in the ERP domain, delivering Dynamics AX advisory and solutions
Company Size	40+ employees (end 2017), and growing
Global Presence	Two offices in Denmark, one in Dubai. Considering opening more offices in Denmark and abroad

Back in 2008 two Danes, Anders Nielsen and Henrik Berg Andersen, founded Pingala with the idea of creating a company they would want to work in for the rest of their professional careers.

Both had personal experiences from long engagements with customers, delivering IT solutions to the ERP market. Both agreed on what they had learned from these engagements.

They now wanted to create something that fitted them perfectly, for the rest of their lives. They wanted great teamwork, fruitful dialogue with customers, and a culture acting as a lever for relation-based collaboration. They wanted high expertise. They also wanted no oversold or derailed projects, and fair compensation and salary.

With that in mind, Anders Nielsen and Henrik Berg Andersen founded Pingala, with culture and competency as the two bearing points.

This goal became the litmus test for decisions and actions going forward, as they steadily grew, got more customers and colleagues, and a board of directors. And, when Kent Højlund was engaged as CEO in 2013, they all jointly put even more focus on the culture, and asked:

"How can we firmly scale the company, AND stay true to the original idea of a company that we would want to work in for the rest of our professional careers?

And in what ways do we need to differentiate ourselves with regards to our ecosystem, our partners, our delivery mechanisms, and culture – both to attract the right talent, and to beat competition?

How can we create a 'Blue Ocean' in an otherwise Red Sea?"

An amplification and further vitalisation of the original idea was underway, with the key role models as active and participating catalysts.

NURTURING THE IDEA OF A MODERN WORKPLACE

During this continuous exploration, the employees in Pingala began fleshing out the details of the journey that they were on, inspired from personal learning, from case stories in the media, and from international disrupters. To a greater extent, they began formulating their modern workplace, and the guiding principles that they wanted to activate.

At that time, in the middle of the 2010-decade, very few Danish companies were working with this kind of organizational design, hence Pingala had to invent, inspect and adapt their own approaches and mechanisms frequently, and with the right timing. All of this was not without debate, learning, mistakes, and changes, but at the same time with huge wins and always a 'people first' mindset.

One thing that became clear, was that to be part of Pingala you needed to have the will, skill, and ability to experiment and change. This change was to a large extent headed by the founders, who, from time to time, stated that they *were* out of their comfort zone, but were absolutely interested and curious to keep pushing the boundaries of their perception of an 'organization'. All these key role models had a huge influence on the cohesiveness of the culture, and on the adoption of new ideas.

During this period, a Pingala mission statement was formulated: **"An oasis for the market's most talented Dynamics 365 people for the benefit of our customers in a lifelong cooperation."** Note the serendipitous adaptation of the triple-bottom-line of responsive leadership in the mission statement: focus on social capital and value-creation to support economic health.

Much of what they subconsciously and intuitively did – and continue to do – is in line with five guiding principles of the future of work.

Their journey over the past decade has seen them start to work with their mechanisms in a conscious way. They are very much aware of their initiatives and actions, yet they keep experimenting. Pingala is increasingly becoming consciously competent, and the notion of the modern workplace is a clear goal for all employees.

HANDLING CULTURE AS A PRODUCT

Wanting to move away from the traditional mindset and thinking, processes, staffing rules, politics, sales routines, payment models, and administrative overheads, Pingala gradually redesigned their approach to work.

Initially, it was not a design parameter to avoid middle managers, but the idea of having a totally flat organization with no middle managers was the result of research on the AX-market, seeking a way to differentiate from competitors regarding customer approach, employee approach, organisational structure, and capacity costs of operation. Steadily it became a key point of the internal mindset of Pingala, and such strong culture intuitively calls for distributed leadership-followership, and shared responsibility for actions and success.

This meant that all the traditional processes were on the list for evaluation in the light of the flat organization: how to hire the right people, how to manage mechanisms like salary and bonus adjustments, how to develop and take care of the employees, and how to deliver valuable and profitable customer projects. All of this should be handled with decentralised leadership and shared responsibility.

A few years after the formulation of the mission statement, the term **'our culture is our product'** was born. For an IT company, this is a radically different way of thinking, but it is exactly the way Pingala wanted the employees to address the oasis and the culture. This had two implications:

Firstly, that the mindset should embrace the fact that culture is a thing that Pingala produces and identifies itself by. Culture as a product is clearly 'Blue Ocean', and attracts attention from potential colleagues, customers, and partners.

Secondly, that culture should be guided by a roadmap, with actions and projects, with shared engagement, and with a steady rhythm for progress, just as classic IT products and deliveries are.

To obtain this, several frequent activities have been launched, of which only a few will be listed here.

PURPOSE AND MEANINGFULNESS

Pingala has a long habit of spending 8-10 full days annually on company-wide workshops, focusing on one or more aspects of the mechanisms of the company, be they culture or business.

A key activity at one such workshop was a visualisation exercise to let the employees imagine and vocalise their future in Pingala, and the feeling they experience by looking some two, four, ten years ahead. Sharing those expectations with each other clearly created a bond, and has become a part of the company memory that they revisit regularly.

Other workshops have touched upon the purpose, meaningfulness, and the value they create for the customers and themselves, and on understanding the differences in approach to strategy, innovation, culture, identity, and distributed leadership.

At almost every workshop this has spawned activities that have been handled on the company-wide Scrum board with an agile approach to execution.

SOCIAL CAPITAL AND THE NETWORKED MECHANISMS

One very central element for Pingala is the social capital. This includes understanding it, measuring it and nurturing it. An organizational network analysis (ONA) was conducted twice, with a year in between, to map the employee relationships on four dimensions: collaboration, sparring, energy, and non-professional relationship. This was used to strengthen the quality and frequency of the dialogue and feedback across Pingala.

More radically, it paved the way for peer-to-peer network-based mentor-arrangements. They were nicknamed KNUS (Danish for 'hug'): KNUS is an acronym for

'Kollega-Netværks-Udviklings-Samtale', which translates as colleague network development conversation.

With one of the guiding principles being the notion of a flat organization with no middle managers, there was a need to remove the CEO from the traditional hub-and-spoke development conversations, and replace it with a network based mechanism. From a practical perspective, it's not possible for a manager to have one-to-one meetings with 40+ employees within a reasonable timeframe. From a mindset perspective, network-based peer-to-peer mentoring is in line with the idea of distributed leadership.

Based on the findings in the ONA, a list of mentor/mentee-pairs were created. Guided by the principles of the networked approach, a third employee, who worked with the mentee on a daily basis, was also assigned to each pair to act as a bystander. The mentor team meets 4-6 times annually, to serve as the central feedback and development mechanism for the mentee.

In this setup, budgeting and funding for education and development activities is handled locally by the mentor/mentee groups; as such, mandate is provided to the KNUS participants in line with the mindset. There has never been an issue with overspending or using funding in a non-collegial manner, as the employees manage the responsibility as if the resources are their own. On the contrary, this has at times led to underspending, and has required encouragement to remember to use the funding.

Naturally, the CEO was part of this mechanism on the same level as everybody else, and contributed both as mentor for an employee, and was assigned a mentor himself. By removing the manager as the central gravity point for all employee development, and instead engaging peer coaching at eye level, a whole new commitment and outcome was obtained.

The results of this peer-to-peer mentoring were clear. The mentees got sparring and feedback from colleagues at eyelevel, and the mentors were just as happy with the setup as the mentees, as it gave them the feeling of giving back.

The idea of having a team or group of employees to handle the different critical mechanisms was copied to the customer engagement routine, where a 'Customer-HUG' was designed. The primary goal was the same as for the KNUS: to engage in a network based mechanism, as a replacement for the traditional Key Account Management and sales-department-thinking. The intention was to keep sales activities as a concern and responsibility of all employees. The Customer-HUG was designed with a flexible regularity, but with two fixed components: a customer advisory board with relevant employees from Pingala, and a template to keep the business development and innovation ideas flowing, focusing on the value to be delivered.

RESULTS AND OUTCOME

It is clear what has made Pingala successful in this journey towards a modern workplace:

- Charismatic key role models, who can establish followership
- A strong motivation to engage in the development journey
- Few, but clear, design principles, leading away from the traditional organization towards future of work
- Engaged employees
- A continued focus on culture
- A strict supervision of the network based mechanisms
- A willingness to experiment, inspect, and adapt.

The results become clear in all three elements of the triple-bottom-line of modern workplaces:
- Strong social capital within the organization
- High rate of perceived value, as reported by the customers
- Exponential growth in turnover and revenue.

Pingala has become an attractive organization, both for existing and potential candidates, and for the customers they engage with.

Clearly – and as an integrated part of the philosophy behind Pingala – all employees need to be involved and engaged in this work. As the organization grows and evolves, new employees with new approaches to work and collaboration enter the scene and influence the shared dynamics of the culture. Continuous reinforcement of the mindset and mechanisms are needed, driven by the key role models.

WHAT NOW?

Pingala is a modern workplace that aligns with the five guiding principles of future of work.

Looking at the history of Pingala and the inertia of the transition towards the future of work, there is no sign of slowing down.

Over the years, Pingala has grown from two to 40+ employees, and from below $0.5million to above $7million in gross profit. As a token of the steady growth, Pingala has achieved the Danish Gazelle award five years consecutively. (The Gazelle award is established by the Danish financial paper Børsen, and is given to organizations who over four consecutive years – amongst other things – have continuous growth, and at least doubled their revenue.)

The growth in social capital, value-creation, and financials is steady, and there is clearly a pathway to being maybe

100 employees across multiple locations and countries within a few years.

The question is: is that what Pingala wants?

On multiple occasions it has been said that if the growth dismantles or disrupts the culture, the employees will leave. Pingala should be an oasis; a company, that employees would want to work in for the rest of their lives.

Growth is not a goal in itself. The oasis of Pingala is the goal.

13
CASE STUDY: PROACTIVE
– A COMPANY THAT PEOPLE RETURN TO

COMPANY CHARACTERISTICS

Company Name	ProActive A/S
Industry	IT consultancy, providing advisory and solutions to SMB and enterprise companies based on the Microsoft stack
Company Size	Approaching 200 employees (2017), and growing
Global Presence	Four offices in Denmark

Many things are said by the employees about the culture and leadership in ProActive:

"I was in for a tough start. Full speed ahead, and it was up to me to define my role."

"With so many possibilities and opportunities, it took me a while to understand my contribution."

"Once I 'got it', it was like releasing a buffer of energy."

"Wow, those people really care about me, and they know my personal motivation and interests."

In many aspects, this resembles the tales told by employees in companies with deeply rooted and omnipresent cultural traits; which is exactly what characterises ProActive:

- A clear goal and mission
- A leadership that enables others to take lead
- Responsibility and high expectations
- A lot of engagement mechanisms, and only a few stringent structures and procedures
- A team-of-teams organization
- A drive for results, value-creation, and economic health.

Over the years, this has led to significant results, on all elements of the modern bottom-line:

- Constantly high employee satisfaction
- Decreasing absenteeism and sick leave, from above 4.5% to below 2.6%
- Growing number of employees: from five to nearly 200 employees as of end 2017
- Financial growth: $27million in revenue, as of end 2017.

The most interesting result, however, is that **people return to ProActive**:

For every five employees who leave ProActive, two return within a few years.

Why? Because of the culture, they say.

BUILDING A COMPANY THAT PEOPLE RETURN TO

Culture is solely built from behaviour, which is shaped and nurtured by the surrounding leadership.

In 1997, Claus Topholt and Max Sejbæk founded ProActive in its initial form, with technological development as a springboard: the internet and digitalisation was in rapid development.

Within a few years, the core leadership group was in place; a C-level team that still remain in the company. Also, significant investment was obtained from prominent Danish 'business angels' and companies.

From the beginning, the mission has been clear: 'Thinking Your Business', a term that coins the approach to providing value to customers and each other, and to solving problems. Never bluntly apply an approach, a piece of technology, or a pre-cooked solution; always look at the problem from the receiver's end, thinking of *their* business.

The entire leadership group and the managers in ProActive are characterised by living this mission vividly, and by being role models in mindset, skillset, and behaviour. Even in situations where the company has made major mistakes in approach to a solution, the leadership group has stood up to their promise and showed through their actions what matters to them and to the company.

What also stands out is the applied situational leadership. There are high expectations as to engagement and quality, both within the organization and towards customers. With an 'I trust that you can do it' mindset, the responsibility and accountability is rapidly given to the employees, in accordance with the will, skill, and experience of said employee. This is distributed leadership in a nutshell, where the employee is required to take part in shaping their role and contribution, and the leader supports with a situational mix-and-dose of instruction and motivation.

Naturally, when this kind of empowerment and meritocracy-based authority replaces micro-management, mistakes can happen. In those cases, both leaders and employees step up rapidly to help each other. Again, this is a characteristic of the culture.

Leadership shapes behaviour, and behaviour shapes culture. All five of the guiding principles of the future of work are motioned in ProActive:

1. People first
2. Purpose, meaning, sense-making, and value-creation
3. Continuous innovation and experimentation
4. An insatiable drive for results
5. Everybody has the opportunity to take a lead.

MECHANISMS FOR RUNNING A COMPANY THAT PEOPLE RETURN TO

Throughout the years, 'involvement' has been a recurrent theme when it comes to major decisions. Naturally, this has been applied with varying breadth, but wanting to run a business with engaged employees requires that you involve the key influencers and role models in tactical and strategic activities in some form.

The strategic direction has often been established by a rather wide group of key influencers and change agents across the organization, leading to a tactical breakdown of activities with the involvement of everyone.

ProActive has also experimented with a strategy execution based on the principles from Agile and Scrum, with a sprint length of one month, leading to a tripling of actual completed activities.

Speaking of Scrum, ProActive was one of the first IT companies in Denmark to embrace and apply Scrum on a company-wide basis; an approach that has become the heartbeat of the delivery process.

This has also lead to a networked team-of-teams organization. Over the years, several matrix-like structures have been used, either oriented towards technologies, services, or industries. Across this matrix, delivery teams have been formed, who organized themselves in accordance with the Agile roles.

ProActive has even experimented with local, full-service industry teams, in line with the possibility of self-management in a team-of-teams approach.

To get an understanding of the organizational mechanisms and dynamics, a network analysis (ONA) has been conducted twice, to highlight the collaboration across the organization and across locations too, and to nurture the responsiveness.

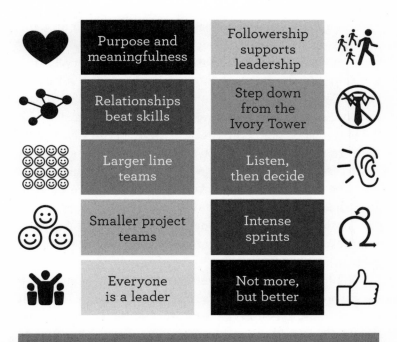

FIGURE 48

The 10 characteristics of a modern workplace, which ProActive fully comply with

The key to obtaining this kind of responsive organization on top of the strong empowerment has been a deliberate investment in horizontal leadership. Bringing the
approximately 20 peer leaders together in cross-organizational forums regularly to get to know each other and to
share challenges and experiences has been a huge lever for
the social capital. These meetings have taken place weekly
in the local offices, and quarterly on a company level. Also,
a lot of ad-hoc one-to-one meetings are held between peer
managers. This has further strengthened the ability to
respond to changes in technology, with customers, and in
employees' desires for development.

One of the key mechanisms for running such an agile
and responsive organization is a frequent way of cou-
pling employees with the tasks to be done. Every Friday,
a resource assignment meeting is held between all delivery-responsible employees and line managers, with the
purpose of matching employees to projects and tasks. The
delivery-responsible employees, who are typically project
managers, request a role to be filled or a task to be executed.
In rare cases, they request a specific employee to their team.
The line managers then have the responsibility for making
sure that the employees get the tasks that they dream of,
are motivated by, and can develop with. This, of course,
requires the line manager to have a deep understanding of
each employee.

The 'people first' approach also shines through in the
hiring process. It takes a long time, and it's handled by both
the line managers and the colleagues of the potential candidate. Since culture is prominent in ProActive, the attitude
and mindset is a compelling factor for the decisions.

Likewise, letting people go is handled with the employee
in mind. If it becomes clear that the employee and ProActive have grown apart, the line manager holds a meeting

with the employee with exactly that message: "We've grown apart. Let's find a solution." If this means that the paths separate, the line manager often will strive to help the employee into a good, new job.

LEADERSHIP THAT PEOPLE RETURN TO

It's interesting to observe that all four of the roles of a responsive leader are present among the leaders in ProActive:

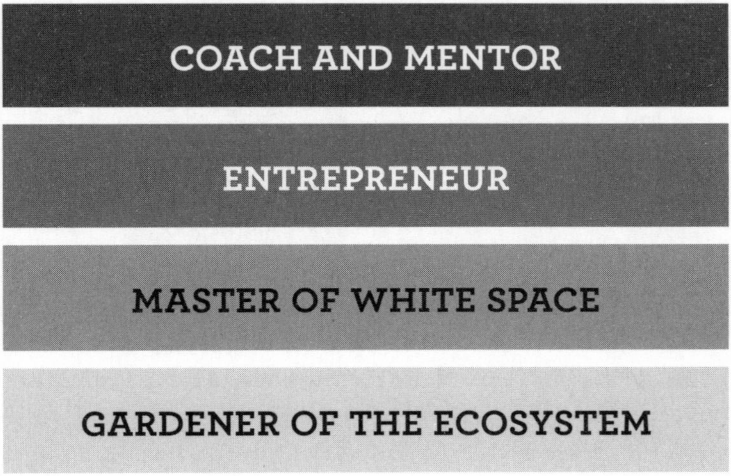

COACH AND MENTOR

ENTREPRENEUR

MASTER OF WHITE SPACE

GARDENER OF THE ECOSYSTEM

FIGURE 49

The four roles of the responsive leaders in ProActive

Likewise, all eight behaviours are motioned and nurtured across the leaders and managers:

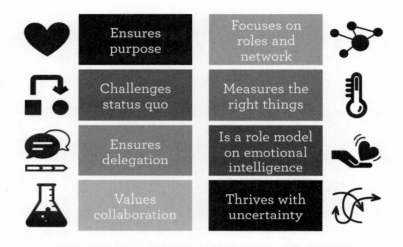

FIGURE 50

The eight behaviours of the responsive leaders in ProActive

Some of the leaders have it in them as a natural gift. Some of the leaders use the input and ability of each other to master the roles and behaviour together.

The result is that people return to ProActive.

REFERENCES

Agile Alliance. 2001. *The Agile Manifesto*. Agile Alliance. http://agilemanifesto.org/.

Aversa, Paolo, Alessandro Marino, Luiz Mesquita, and Jaideep Anand. 2015. *Driving Performance via Exploration in Changing Environments: Evidence from Formula One Racing*. Informs PubsOnLine. 25 May. http://pubsonline.informs.org/doi/abs/10.1287/orsc.2015.0984.

Aversa, Paolo, and Scott Berinato. 2017. "Sometimes, Less Innovation Is Better." *Harvard Business Review*, May-June. http://www.iesep.com/en/sometimes-less-innovation-is-better-137294.html.

Bailey, Catherine, and Adrian Madden. 2016. *What Makes Work Meaningful — Or Meaningless*. MIT Sloan Management Review. June. http://sloanreview.mit.edu/article/what-makes-work-meaningful-or-meaningless/.

Bain & Company. 2016. "The Elements Of Value." *Harvard Business Review*, September.

Bcorporation.net. 2017. *bcorporation.net*. https://www.bcorporation.net/.

Belbin, Meredith R. 1993. *Team Roles at work*. Elsevier Ltd.

Bersin. 2017. *Bersin by Deloitte*. http://home.bersin.com/.

Bloch, Line. 2016. *An easy way to measure employee happiness*. Bloch&Østergaard. http://blochoestergaard.dk/employee-happiness/.

Caulkin, Simon. 2016. *Companies with a purpose beyond profit tend to make more money*. http://on.ft.com/2xKB06v.

CEB. 2017. *Three Steps to Build an Ideation Process*. CEB. July. https://www.cebglobal.com/blogs/research-development-three-steps-to-build-an-ideation-process/.

Center for Futures Studies. 2017. *SCENARIO Magazine*. www.scenariomagazine.com.

Christensen, Clayton M. 1997. *The Innovator's Dilemma: The Revolutionary Book That Will Change the Way You Do Business.* New York: Harvard Business Essentials.

Conscious Capitalism. 2017. *Conscious Capitalism.* https://www.consciouscapitalism.org/.

Covey, Stephen R. 1989. *The 7 Habits of Highly Effective People.* New York: Free Press.

Danske Bank. 2015. *Our Leadership Book.* Danske Bank.

de Montjoye, Yves-Alexandre, Arkadiusz Stopczynski, Erez Shmueli, Alex Pentland, and Sune Lehmann. 2014. "The Strength of the Strongest Ties in Collaborative Problem Solving." *Nature Scientific Reports*, June.

Deloitte. 2016. *2016 Deloitte Global Human Capital Trends.* Deloitte.

Deloitte. 2017. *2017 Deloitte Global Human Capital Trends.* Deloitte.

Denning, Steve. 2011. *Peggy Noonan On Steve Jobs And Why Big Companies Die.* Forbes. Nov. http://bit.ly/2xTD8L6.

Ebdrup, Allan. 2017. *Allan Ebdrup, LinkedIn.* https://www.linkedin.com/in/ebdrup/.

Edmondson, Amy C. 2012. *Teaming: How Organizations Learn, Innovate, and Compete in the Knowledge Economy.* Harvard Business School.

Ernst, Barron. 2017. *How product managers are slowly becoming mini CEOs.* The Next Web. http://bit.ly/2hGTCMS.

Forbes. 2017. *Forbes - make every employee a chief purpose officer.* Forbes. 24 April. http://bit.ly/2xlf3al.

Frey, Carl Benedikt, and Michael A. Osborne. 2013. *The Future Of Employment: How Susceptible are Jobs To Computerisation?* University of Oxford, Oxford School of Economics.

Gallup. 2016. *Employee Engagement in U.S. Stagnant in 2015.* 13 January. http://bit.ly/200qU8Y.

Gallup. 2016. *How Millennials Want to Work and Live.* Gallup.

Goleman, Daniel, and Richard E. Boyatzis. 2017. "Emotional Intelligence Has 12 Elements. Which Do You Need to Work On?" *Harvard Business Review*, February.

Google. 2017. *Learn about Google's manager research.* Google.
https://rework.withgoogle.com/guides/managers-identify-what-
makes-a-great-manager/steps/learn-about-googles-manager-research/.

Goran, Julie, Laura LaBerge, and Ramesh Srinivasan. 2017. "Culture for
a digital age." *McKinsey Quarterly*, July.

Gray, Alex. 2016. *The 10 skills you need to thrive in the Fourth Industrial
Revolution.* World Economic Forum.
https://www.weforum.org/agenda/2016/01/the-10-skills-you-need-
to-thrive-in-the-fourth-industrial-revolution/.

Gray, Dave. 2017. *Empathy Map.* Gamestorming.
http://gamestorming.com/empathy-map/.

Hall, Ali. 2016. *Embracing New Leadership Principles.* Presidents Institute.
https://www.youtube.com/watch?v=xcgiTq-9eII.

Hamel, Gary. 2013. *Hackathon Report - Management Innovation
eXchange.* CIPD and MIX. http://www.managementexchange.com/
sites/default/files/cipd-hr-report-digital.pdf.

Hamel, Gary. 2011. *Reinventing the Technology of Human
Accomplishment.* The University of Phoenix Distinguished
Guest Video Lecture Series. https://www.youtube.com/
watch?v=aodjgkv65MM.

Hansen, Søren Schultz. 2015. *Digitale Indfødte På Job.* Copenhagen:
Gyldendal Business.

Hersey, Paul, and Kenneth H. Blanchard. 1969. *Management of
Organizational Behavior – Utilizing Human Resources.* New Jersey:
Prentice Hall.

Herzberg, Frederick, Bernard Mausner, and Barbara Bloch Snyderman.
1959. *The Motivation to Work.* Wiley & Sons.

Hofstede, Geert. 1980. *Culture's Consequences: International Differences
in Work-Related Values.* SAGE Publications.

Holacracy. 2017. *Holacracy.* http://holacracy.org/.

INSEAD. 2014. *The Four Pillars of Blue Ocean Leadership.* INSEAD.
September. https://knowledge.insead.edu/leadership-
management/the-four-pillars-of-blue-ocean-leadership-3603.

Intuit. 2010. *The Intuit 2020 Report.* Intuit. October.
http://about.intuit.com/futureofsmallbusiness/.

Ismail, Salim, Michael S. Malone, Yuri van Geest, and Peter H. Diamandis. 2014. *Exponential Organizations: Why new organizations are ten times better, faster, and cheaper than yours (and what to do about it)*. New York: Diversion Books.

Jobvite. 2016. *Job Seeker Nation Study*. Jobvite. March. http://bit.ly/2kgk70u.

Kjerulf, Alexander. 2014. *Happy Hour is 9 to 5: How to Love Your Job, Love Your Life, and Kick Butt at Work*. London: Pine Tribe.

Kolind, Lars, and Jacob Bøtter. 2012. *UNBOSS*. Copenhagen: Jyllands-Postens Forlag.

Kotler, Steven, and Peter Diamandis. 2012. *Abundance: The Future Is Better Than You Think*. New York: Free Press.

Krifa. 2016. *God Arbejdslyst Indeks 2016*. Krifa. http://bit.ly/2mLCESg.

Laloux, Frédéric. 2014. *Reinventing Organizations: A Guide to Creating Organizations Inspired by the Next Stage in Human Consciousness*. Brussels: Nelson Parker.

Lencioni, Patrick. 2002. *The Five Dysfunctions of a Team*. San Francisco: Wiley.

LRN. 2016. "The HOW Report - A Global Empirical Analysis of How Governance, Culture, and Leadership Impact Performance." http://www.pwc.com/gx/en/ceo-agenda/pulse/purpose.html.

Maister, David H., Robert Galford, and Charles Green. 2000. *The Trusted Advisor*. The Free Press.

Markides, Constantinos C. 2015. *How to Succeed by Breaking the Rules in Your Business*. Presidents Institute. http://bit.ly/2xPH7bo.

McGinn, Daniel. 2017. "The Science of Pep Talks." *Harvard Business Review*, July-August.

McKinsey. 2017. *A future that works: The impact of automation in Denmark*. McKinsey. April. http://bit.ly/2pso0QJ.

Mikkelsen, Kenneth, and Richard Martin. 2016. *THE NEO-GENERALIST: Where you go is who you are*. London: LID Publishing.

Minor, Dylan, and Jan W. Rivkin. 2016. *Truly Human Leadership at Barry-Wehmiller*. Harvard Business Review.

Minzberg, Henry, Joseph B. Lampel, James Brian Quinn, and Sumantra Ghoshal. 1988. *The Strategy Process: Concepts, Contexts, Cases.* Trans-Atlantic Publications.

Mogensen, Klaus Æ., Jacob Suhr Thomsen, Niels Bøttger Rasmussen, Monica H. Traxl, Carsten Beck, and Christine Lind Ditlevsen. 2009. *Anarchonomy.* Instituttet for Fremtidsforskning.

Mogensen, Klaus Æ., Kim Møller-Elshøj, Jacob Suhr THomsen, Cecilie Brøndum Boesen, Sara Jönsonn, and Matthew Tanner Richards. 2010. *Ude af Kontrol.* Instituttet for Fremtidsforskning.

Morgan, Jacob. 2015. *The Complete Guide To The 5 Types Of Organizational Structures For The Future Of Work.* July. https://thefutureorganization.com/the-complete-guide-to-the-5-types-of-organizational-structures-for-the-future-of-work/.

Morgan, Jacob. 2017. *The Employee Experience Advantage.* New York: Wiley & Sons.

OfficeVibe. 2017. *The Best Employee Engagement Resources.* OfficeVibe. https://www.officevibe.com/resources.

Peters, Tom. 2015. *Excellence Now: Action.*

Pink, Daniel H. 2009. *Drive: The surprising truth about what motivates us.* Edinburgh, London, New York, Melbourne: Canongate.

Putnam, Robert D. 2000. *Bowling Alone: The Collapse and Revival of American Community.* New York: Simon & Schuster Paperbacks.

PWC. 2016. *Connecting the dots: how purpose can join up your business.* PWC. http://www.pwc.com/gx/en/ceo-agenda/pulse/purpose.html.

Reichheld, Frederick F. 2003. "The One Number You Need to Grow." *Harvard Business Review,* December. https://hbr.org/2003/12/the-one-number-you-need-to-grow.

Responsive.Org. 2017. *Responsive Org.* http://www.responsive.org/.

Ries, Eric. 2011. *The Lean Startup.* New York: Crown Business.

Rozovsky, Julia. 2015. *The five keys to a successful Google team.* Google. https://rework.withgoogle.com/blog/five-keys-to-a-successful-google-team/.

Rummler, Geary A., and Alan P. Brache. 1990. *Improving Performance: How to Manage the White Space on the Organization Chart*. San Francisco: Jossey-Bass.

Sak, Paul J. 2017. "The Neuroscience of Trust." *Harvard Business Review*, January. https://hbr.org/2017/01/the-neuroscience-of-trust.

Seligman, Martin. 2011. *Flourish - A Visionary New Understanding of Happiness and Well-Being*. New York: Free Press.

Sheridan, Richard. 2013. *Joy, Inc.: How We Built a Workplace People Love*. London: Penguin Random House.

WorldBlu. 2014. *Leaders Eat Last: Why Some Teams Pull Together and Others Don't*. Portfolio / Penguin.

WorldBlu. 2009. *Start With Why*. London: Penguin.

Singularity University. 2017. *Global Grand Challenges*. Singularty University. https://su.org/about/global-grand-challenges/.

Skov, Søren. 2017. *Søren Skov, LinkedIn*. https://www.linkedin.com/in/srenskov/.

Spork, Maz. 2017. *Maz Spork, LinkedIn*. https://www.linkedin.com/in/mazspork/.

Stewart, Henry. 2012. *The Happy Manifesto: Make Your Organization a Great Workplace*. London: Kogan Page.

Strategyzer AG. 2017. *The Business Model Canvas*. Strategyzer AG. https://strategyzer.com/canvas/business-model-canvas.

Strategyzer AG. 2017. *The Value Proposition Canvas*. Strategyzer AG. https://strategyzer.com/canvas/value-proposition-canvas.

Sutherland, Jeff. 2014. *Scrum: The Art of Doing Twice the Work in Half the Time*. RH Business Books.

Tuckman, Bruce W. 1965. "Developmental sequence in small groups." *Psychological Bulletin*.

UN. 2017. *UN Sustainable Goals*. United Nations. http://www.un.org/sustainabledevelopment/sustainable-development-goals/.

Vickberg, Suzanne M. Johnson, and Kim Christfort. 2017. "The New Science of Team Chemistry." *Harvard Business Review*, March. https://hbr.org/2017/03/the-new-science-of-team-chemistry.

WD-40. 2017. *Our Tribal Culture.* WD-40.
https://www.wd40company.com/careers/our-tribal-culture/.

Morgan, Jacob. 2017. *Diffusion of innovations.* Wikipedia.
http://bit.ly/1PhwzDX.

Morgan, Jacob. 2017. *Emotional intelligence.* http://bit.ly/1MV8sYx.

Morgan, Jacob. 2017. *Scrum (software development).* http://bit.
ly/1Ccrqmo.

Morgan, Jacob. 2017. *Social capital.* Wikipedia. http://bit.ly/2gFOWr8.

Morgan, Jacob. 2017. *Volatility, uncertainty, complexity and ambiguity.*
http://bit.ly/1JhAIWk.

World Economic Forum. 2017. *World Economic Forum.* World Economic
Forum. https://www.weforum.org/.

WorldBlu. 2015. *Freedom At Work: Growth And Resilience.* WorldBlu.

WorldBlu. 2017. *WorldBlu.* http://worldblu.com/.

YoungConsult. 2017. *#Youngster - 5 dogmer til at tiltrække og fastholde
Millennials.* Copenhagen.

Ørsted, Christian. 2013. *Livsfarlig Ledelse.* Pine Tribe Limited.

Østergaard, Kris, and Erik Korsvik Østergaard. 2016. *Does
your co-worker want your boss to be a robot?* DARE2 and
Bloch&Østergaard. August. http://dare2.dk/future-of-work/.

Aakerberg, Michelle Czajkowski. 2016. *SCENARIO Magazine.* SCENARIO.
http://www.scenariomagazine.com/your-childrens-jobs-have-yet-
to-be-invented/.

AN INTRODUCTION TO
ERIK KORSVIK ØSTERGAARD

Erik Korsvik Østergaard (M.Sc.) is a trusted advisor, and has worked as manager, project manager, and consultant for nearly 20 years, focusing more and more on leadership, change management and organisational development.

Erik has a burning passion for the future of work and the ongoing paradigm shift in leadership. He has specific experience with new leadership practices in daily life and cross-cultural setups, and has developed several tools to implement it – with strong, measurable results.

He acts as key note speaker, change driver, and mentor. In addition, he's a keen jazz pianist.